ALPHAVILLE

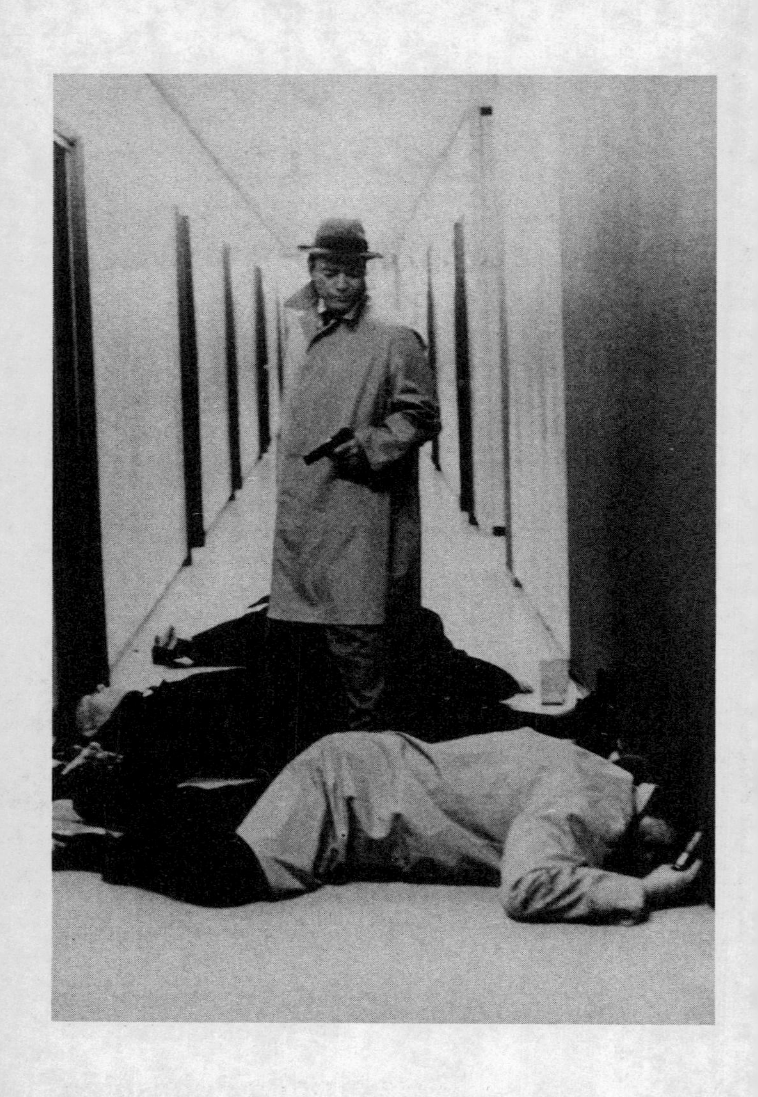

CLASSIC
FILM
SCRIPTS

ALPHAVILLE

a film by

Jean-Luc Godard

English translation of screenplay
by Peter Whitehead

Lorrimer Publishing

First published in 1972 by
Lorrimer Publishing Incorporated, UK, 1972; Revised edition 1984
Publisher and Editor: Andrew Sinclair

This edition first published in 2000
by Faber and Faber Limited
3 Queen Square London WC1N 3AU

Printed in England

A CIP record for this book
is available from the British Library

ISBN 0-571-20633-6

10 9 8 7 6 5 4 3 2 1

CONTENTS:

ACKNOWLEDGEMENTS

I should like to thank M. Jean-Luc Godard for giving *carte-blanche* permission for the description of the action of the film. He shot the film on the basis of the Treatment and only afterwards, largely to assist the sub-title work, was the dialogue put down on paper.

I wish to thank Mr George Hoellering of the Academy Cinema, who distributes the film in this country, and Monsieur Vogtens of Transocean-Eximport, without whose efforts this publication would not have been possible.

For assistance in the translation I wish to thank Monsieur Marcel Petit, Madame Genevieve Petit and Alexis Lykiard.

CREDITS:

Written & Directed by	Jean-Luc Godard
Photography	Raoul Coutard
Music	Paul Misraki
Editor	Agnes Guillemot
Sound	René Levert
Producer	André Michelin

A Chaumiane-Filmstudio production, distributed in England by Academy Cinema Ltd.

CAST:

Lemmy Caution	Eddie Constantine
Natasha von Braun	Anna Karina
Professor von Braun	Howard Vernon
Henry Dickson	Akim Tamiroff
Chief Engineer	Laszlo Szabo

CERTIFICATE : 'A'   RUNNING TIME : 98 mins

For J

Introduction

ANGUISH : ALPHAVILLE

Lemmy Caution : ' Never forget that Revenger and Reporter begin with the same letter.'

It is seventeen minutes past midnight, Oceanic Time; having driven all night through intersidereal space, secret agent Lemmy Caution — disguised as Ivan Johnson, reporter for Figaro-Pravda — arrives in the suburbs of Alphaville. The road is empty, the night grey; Lemmy is alone, with only a revolver in the glove compartment.

* * *

Thus begins *Alphaville*, or *A Strange Adventure of Lemmy Caution*. Another title Godard wanted to use was ' Tarzan versus IBM ', and the first time I saw *Alphaville* it was the pop art aspect of the film that struck me most.

Of course, Godard, like Marker and Resnais, has been intrigued by comic strips for many years before the term pop art existed. Comic strips seem to represent many things for Godard : first, a source book for the contemporary collective subconscious; secondly, a dramatic framework derived from modern myth — in much the same way as Joyce used the Ulysses myth; thirdly, a reaction against the subtleties of the psychological novel; finally, the attraction of comic strip narrative with its sudden shifting of scene, its freedom of narration, its economy.

The plot of *Alphaville* is pure sci-fi comic strip; Caution (Eddie Constantine) has been sent to Alphaville, city of the future, to bring back or kill Professor von Braun, architect of this capital of computers. Three agents have already failed : Dick Tracy, Flash Gordon, and Henri Dickson. Caution eventually succeeds in his mission, even managing to carry off Natasha von Braun (Anna Karina), to whom he succeeds in teaching the meaning of love. The Robot has been redeemed.

Just like a Lichtenstein painting ('Oh, Brad, [*gulp*] it should have been that way'), the dialogue often echoes the balloons. 'Let this serve as a warning to all those who try to . . .' etc. Characterisation, too, has been reduced to a minimum. The musical score, by Paul Misraki, is extremely effective as used by Godard, but in itself it is (intentionally) the nearest he could get to the Max Steiner of the 1930s. Furthermore, Godard uses all the typographical symbols beloved of pop artists — arrows, buttons, neon lights — all the signposts of modern life.

But *Alphaville* doesn't look like a comic strip, and this is where Godard diverges from the true pop artist, who has been defined as 'a man who offers a coincidence of style and subject, one who represents mass-produced images and objects in a style which is also based upon the visual vocabulary of mass production'. In other words, the pop artist not only likes the fact of his commonplace objects but, more important, exults in their commonplace look. Godard resembles much more pop fringe figures like Larry Rivers and Rauschenberg who, although fascinated by pop imagery, translate it into a non-pop style.

The second time I saw *Alphaville*, it was precisely the great refinement and plastic beauty of its style that impressed me. Like the volume of Eluard poems which the dying Henri Dickson (Akim Tamiroff) presses into Lemmy's hand, Alphaville is the Capital of Pain (*Capitale de la Douleur*), and the visual style of the film is painful, menacing, anxiety-ridden. Alphaville is Paris. The swimming pool where the intractable citizens are machine-gunned and finished off by knife-wielding girls in bikinis is actually on the outskirts of Paris. The new Electricity Board building is one of the computer centres; the hotel where Lemmy stays is the Scribe near the Place de

l'Opéra. The problem was to film Paris to make it look like the city of Alpha 60, the city whose inhabitants have become the slaves of electronic probabilities, where tranquillisers come with every hotel room, and logic and the eternal present reign.

On the other hand there was no real problem, for Paris has always been for Godard the Capital of Pain, and his style has always been anguish-ridden. Without trick shots and special effects, menace is rendered in the usual Godard/Coutard fashion: avoidance of extra lighting creates not an effect of realism, but of a city where the blackness is stronger than the occasional pools of light. Again, because he does not generally use special lighting, he can make play with reflection and shadow in a manner which cannot always be planned in advance, but which always gives the same inevitable effect of mysterious dread. One cannot be sure that individual shots in a Godard film have been planned to create a special dramatic effect, but they always contribute to the mood and general tenor of the film. For example, the glass-enclosed lift in Lemmy's hotel is the excuse for some fabulously disturbing reflection effects. These are beautiful in themselves, but I don't think they have any specific relevance at the moment we see them. On the other hand, the ambiguity of the reflections, the fact that we are often unsure of where the camera could have been placed, are of course an effective mirroring of Lemmy's *dépaysement* and fears.

As befits a study of a totalitarian State, much of the film takes place in long bureaucratic corridors, labyrinths of power, mazes at whose centre lies death. Here again, Coutard's flat underlighting and the graininess of the image render the East Berlin effect in all its greyness and desperation. But the palaces of the government, on the other hand, are all sinister elegance, more like New York. In the same way, the northern suburbs are covered in snow and ice, while the southern suburbs are hot and steamy.

* * *

For *Alphaville* is built visually on extreme contrasts, or so I realised more fully the third time I saw it. Basically there is the contrast of the straight line and the circle. For Godard, the circle represents evil: a man must go straight ahead, says the condemned man on the diving-board. So everything in Alphaville that represents the tyranny of the computers is circular. Lemmy's hotel suite is built in circular form; the staircases in the government buildings are spiral; even the city itself is, like Paris, circular, and to get from one place to another one must take a circular route. The corridors may be straight, but one always ends up where one started. And of course the computers move in circles. Time, says Alpha 60, is an endless circle. Lemmy, however, maintains that all one has to do is to go straight ahead towards everything one loves, straight ahead: when one arrives at the goal, one realises that one has nevertheless come full circle.

The inhabitants of Alphaville even talk in circles. Whenever anyone says hello, the reply is invariable: 'Very well, thank you, please.' 'You must never say *why*; only *because*,' admonishes Natasha. Death and life are inscribed in the same hopeless circle.

Contrast is also displayed in Godard's treatment of the sound. The main musical theme is, as I have said, syrupy and romantic, but it never gets beyond the introductory cadence. And it is inter-cut with harsh discordant noises: the slamming of doors, the whirling of the computers, and, worst of all, the electronic grating voice of Alpha 60, which is as unpleasant as it is indescribable. It would sound like a death-rattle were it not for the absolute evenness and soulless monotony of its delivery. [The sound is not produced electronically. The sound is that of a human voice, but that of a man whose vocal cords were shot away in the war and who has been re-educated to speak from the diaphragm. Godard thought it was important to have, not a mechanical voice, but one which has been, so to speak, killed — like, of course, the inhabitants of Alphaville.]

Godard has always liked to flash brutally from a bright scene to a dark one, but this is carried to extreme proportions in *Alphaville*, where the greyness of the streets is continually contrasted with the blinding floodlights of the electronic nerve centres. Like so many lasers, they torture the brain, at the same time exercising a hypnotic fascination in their rhythmical flashing.

In describing a film as extraordinarily individual as *Alphaville*, it seems somehow an anticlimax to talk about the acting; suffice it to say that Eddie Constantine is the perfect inter-galactic private eye [He's a Martian, says Godard, he's the only one, there isn't any other: that's why I chose him], and that Anna Karina seems to have gone through yet another metamorphosis. Just as the difference between her performances in *Une Femme est une Femme* and *Vivre sa Vie* was incalculably startling, so she had left behind her earlier incarnation, and now stands before us, no longer the wistful little girl of *Bande à Part*, but a woman perfectly capable of rendering both the brainwashed and deadly denizen of Alphaville, and also the woman who can just barely remember life before words like redbreast, autumn light, conscience, tears and tenderness were eradicated from the Bible/Dictionary owned by every inhabitant of Alphaville, new editions of which are distributed daily — as more and more words are forbidden.

* * *

Several times in Godard's career he has produced a film which summed up his previous work, consolidated his advances. *Vivre sa Vie* was such a one; *Alphaville* is another. Now it is quite possible to prefer those films which strike out on new ground, films like *Les Carabiniers* or *Une Femme Mariée*, or, indeed, like *Pierrot le Fou*. Although obviously less perfect, they will be to some more interesting, more exciting. It just depends how much importance one gives to experiment, how much to achievement. To put it differently, whether one prefers romantic striving or classic perfection. I think I have made clear my preference for the latter. The ultimate superiority of *Alphaville* lies not only in its more brilliantly achieved plastic beauty, but in the greater adequacy of its plot — pretext though that plot may be. Without being too pompous about it, one could say that in this film more than in any other, Godard has achieved the most complete degree of correlation between vehicle and content, between style and subject.

RICHARD ROUD

ALPHAVILLE

Screenplay

1

Titles: insistent ominous music: close up full-frame flashing light; a deep, mechanical, monotonous voice intones.

ALPHA 60 : There are times when reality becomes too complex for Oral Communication. But Legend gives it a form by which it pervades the whole world.

Exterior. Night. The suburbs of Alphaville, the Capital City of a distant Galaxy. A lone car is being driven along one of the boulevards, ablaze with flashing lights, neon signs: the city is a complex of light against the night, huge illuminated buildings, a busy metropolis buzzing with an atmosphere of electronic energy.

Close up: LEMMY CAUTION *at the wheel of his white Ford Galaxie. He lights a cigarette as he waits at a traffic signal and transfers his gun from the glove-box into his pocket. A train is silently crossing a long bridge, a bead of light against the darkness, as* LEMMY'S *narration commences.*

LEMMY *off* : It was 24 hours 17 minutes Oceanic Time when I arrived at the suburbs of Alphaville.

Close up: traffic sign. ALPHAVILLE. SILENCE. LOGIC. SAFETY. PRUDENCE.

LEMMY'S *car leaves the busy boulevard and pulls up at the entrance of an hotel. He allows his car to be taken away but rudely refuses to allow his case to be carried by the porter.*

The camera tracks closely behind him as he passes through the multiple glass doors and crosses to the Reception.

LEMMY : My newspaper tele-reserved a room for me.
RECEPTIONIST : Mister?
LEMMY *turning away as he lies* : Ivan Johnson.
RECEPTIONIST : Which newspaper?
LEMMY : Figaro-Pravda.
RECEPTIONIST : That's right . . . Room 344. I presume you've registered at Residents Control? You must, even if only here for the Festival.

A page boy offers to take LEMMY'S *case, but once again he stubbornly refuses to leave go of it.* LEMMY *is taken to the lift and to the second floor. In the lift he puts a cigarette to his lips but, deep in thought, doesn't light it The lift boy holds out his hand for a tip. Instead of giving one,* LEMMY *lights his cigarette and snaps shut his lighter.* LEMMY *is approached by a young woman, who also offers to take his case without success. She leads him along a long, unending corridor towards his room.*

SEDUCTRESS : This way, sir.
Your case, sir.
You're tired, sir?
You'd like to take a little rest . . . sir?
It's this way, sir.
If you're tired you can rest, sir.
It's here, sir.

She talks to LEMMY *in a dull flat monotonous voice, as if she is using words she has learnt before, a formula she must use with all the people she meets. She seems without vitality or emotions. She takes* LEMMY *to his suite of rooms, and* LEMMY *immediately taps the walls, looking for hidden microphones, etc. He goes to the window and looks at the glare of lights and signs outside.*

SEDUCTRESS : The bedroom's through here, sir.
LEMMY : What are you looking for now?
SEDUCTRESS : I'm making sure the Bible's here, sir — everybody has to have one.

LEMMY : Do you believe in that stuff then?
SEDUCTRESS : Yes, of course I do. I'll put your tranquillisers in the bathroom, sir.

She takes the tablets from his bedside table and takes them into the bathroom. LEMMY *follows her, taking off his jacket. Their voices are heard.*

SEDUCTRESS : I'm very well, thank you, not at all. You'll take a bath, sir?
LEMMY : Yes. . . . I've got some thinking to do.
SEDUCTRESS : I'll take your tie then, sir.

While he is in the bathroom, she slips off her overall. Beneath it she is wearing a bra and pants. She leaves the bedroom by a side door and selects a record on the juke-box conveniently placed in the 'juke-box-room' at the side of the bathroom. She joins LEMMY *in the bathroom. As they are talking* LEMMY *flicks the elastic on her pants.*

LEMMY *off* : What's the matter now?
SEDUCTRESS : I'll take a bath with you if you like, sir.
LEMMY : Listen, baby, I'm a big boy now, see, and old enough to find my own dames, so just beat it!

He returns into the bedroom, shrugging his shoulders. He takes a swig from his whisky flask. He has no sooner sat down on the edge of the bed when he hears a man's voice in the bathroom. Reluctantly he goes to investigate.

DETECTIVE *off* : Gotta be polite to the ladies, Mr Johnson!
LEMMY : Merde! . . . What's up now?
DETECTIVE : You don't dig the girl, Mister?
LEMMY : Is she your sister, Mister?

LEMMY *jumps out of the way as the cop takes a dive for him. A fight ensues, during which time* LEMMY'S *assailant manages to smash his fist through two glass walls and a mirror, get himself ducked in the bath with a towel over his head, throws himself through two more glass walls, and finally, as* LEMMY *dives into the bedroom and grabs his gun, gets himself shot dead trying to escape through the door.* LEMMY, *unruffled, shrugs his shoulders again and looks at his smoking gun, disgruntled.*

LEMMY : I'm out of practice.

The SEDUCTRESS *seems equally unmoved by the drama, and tries once again to seduce* LEMMY. *He slaps her face hard.*

SEDUCTRESS : What's that for . . . sir?

LEMMY : What's all this crap! . . . You all junked up or what?

SEDUCTRESS : No, it's all quite normal, sir.

LEMMY : It's just crazy how everything screwy is normal in this crummy town.

LEMMY *tells her to sit down as he wants to take her photograph. She does so, smiling sweetly and seductively at him, smoothing her legs with her hands.* LEMMY *takes flash photographs with his box camera.*

LEMMY *off* : She said her name was Beatrice, Seductress Third Class. I was struck by the sadness and hardness in her face. Definitely something's out of orbit in the Capital of this Galaxy.

LEMMY *takes a nude pin-up from a magazine and makes the girl hold it high over her head/*

A car driving along a street outside in the night/

LEMMY *lying on bed, gun in hand, reading 'THE BIG SLEEP'/*

He fires two shots/

The pin-up nude has two neat holes through her breasts/

Car in street outside.

LEMMY *takes the photograph from the girl and examines it approvingly. She comes up behind him, putting her arms around his neck.*

LEMMY : Not bad for a veteran of Guadalcanal!

SEDUCTRESS : That's just what I was saying to myself about you!

LEMMY : Look, baby, take your billing and cooing out of here, it's a wild goose chase . . . now beat it!

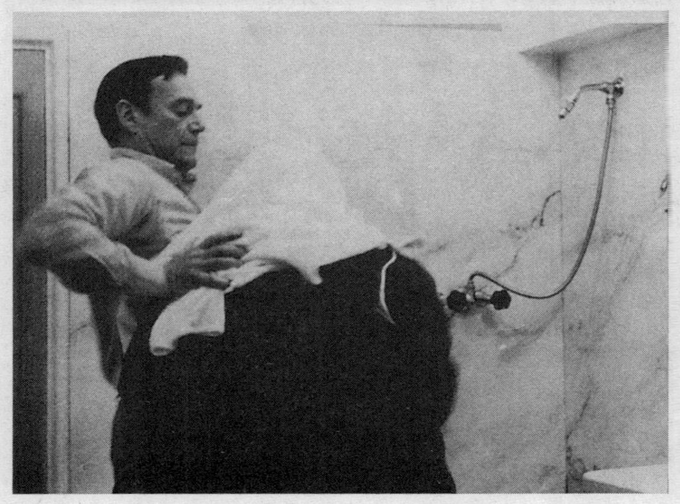

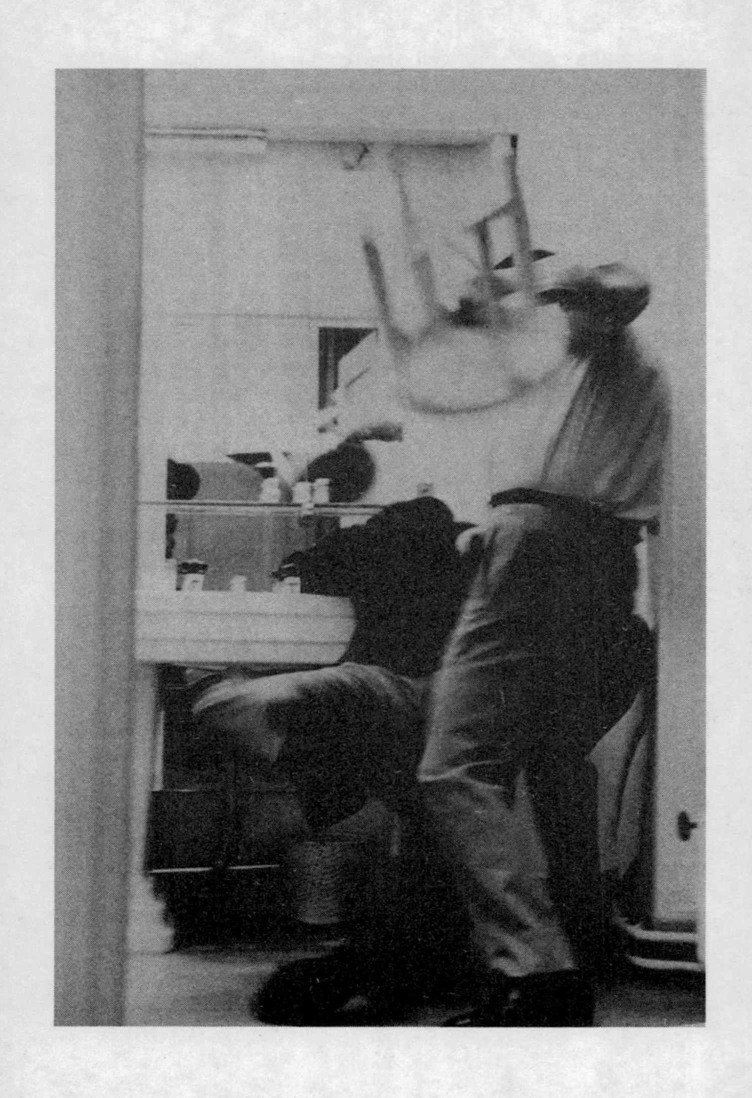

SEDUCTRESS : I'm very well, thank you, not at all.

Having pushed her inelegantly out of the room, LEMMY *ponderously places his cigarette lighter on the mantelpiece. A voice drones out from the intercom device on his bedside table.*

ALPHA 60 : Mr Johnson?

LEMMY : What's the matter now?

Image of huge electrical installation — part of the system comprising ALPHA 60.

ALPHA 60 : Mlle Natasha von Braun.

LEMMY : Who?

ALPHA 60 : . . . is asking for you downstairs.

LEMMY : Just a minute, hold it. . . .

Sitting on the edge of the bed, LEMMY *takes a notebook from his inside pocket, from which he takes snapshots of two men/*

Close up: distinguished man wearing dark glasses/

Back of same photograph; the name Leonard von Braun, Inventor of the Death Ray, α, *alive and liquidate/*

LEMMY *sitting on bed.*

LEMMY : Tell her to wait a minute, I'll be right down.

ALPHA 60 : She is already on her way up.

Close up: photograph of von Braun/

Photograph of other man/

Back of second photograph; Henry Dickson, age 21, 12 rue Enrico Fermi, Alphaville/

LEMMY *swings round and fires a shot, which lights the flame of his cigarette lighter on the mantelpiece . . . as the flame burns, a voice speaks.*

NATASHA : Do you have a light?

LEMMY : Yeh . . . I came 9,000 kilometres to give it to you.

NATASHA : My name is Natasha von Braun.

LEMMY : Yes, I know.

NATASHA : How do you know?

LEMMY : You are Mlle von Braun, aren't you?

NATASHA: Yes. I'm very well, thank you, not at all.

LEMMY *behaves as if he's irritated by the intrusion of this beautiful but mysterious young woman who, like all the others he has met in Alphaville, talks to him in a flat, dull, unemotional voice. As they are talking, he unpacks his case, going into the bathroom with his toothbrush, and he puts his tie back on again.*

NATASHA: You've come from the Outerlands, then, Mr Johnson.

LEMMY: Yeh.

NATASHA: You're comfortable here, I hope.

LEMMY: Yeh, thanks.

NATASHA: I've been ordered to remain at your service throughout your stay at Alphaville.

LEMMY: Who ordered you?

NATASHA: The Authorities, of course. You've come for the Festival, Mr Johnson?

LEMMY: Which Festival?

NATASHA: The Grand Festival! That's why people usually come here from the Outerlands. Frankly, I think it's stupid you didn't come earlier.

LEMMY: Why?

NATASHA: The Festival is nearly over. And there won't be another until some future year.

LEMMY: You're joking — just my luck!

NATASHA: Yes, Mr Johnson. But this evening there's still something, a Gala-Reception — very large — at a Ministry — you can come if you like — I'm going.

LEMMY: O.K. D'accord. But what time? You see, I've something to do beforehand.

NATASHA: Ah! You have to go to Residents Control?

LEMMY: No. What's that?

NATASHA: But you mustn't forget — you have to go there, Mr Johnson. We can meet again afterwards.

LEMMY : No, I'll go along tomorrow. Tonight I've got to see a friend.
NATASHA : I too have work to do this evening. I'll give you the address. We can meet there and go on together afterwards.
LEMMY : O.K. In an hour or two, then.
NATASHA : Until then, Mr Johnson. . . .

LEMMY *decides suddenly to leave with* NATASHA. *He grabs his coat and hat and they leave the room, as the morse-code bleep-bleep of* ALPHA 60 *registers the events somewhere perhaps. . . . Outside the room, a maid is helping* NATASHA *with her coat. They walk together down the corridors, and as they talk, the camera tracks backwards.*

NATASHA : Mr Johnson . . . what is it like in the Outerlands?
LEMMY : You've never been there?
NATASHA : No. When I was a little girl my father used to talk to me about them. But now it's forbidden to even think of them.
LEMMY : Are you often ordered to spend your time with strangers?
NATASHA : Yes, it's my job.
LEMMY : It must be charming sometimes!
NATASHA : Why?
LEMMY : Has no one ever made a pass at you?
NATASHA : What?
LEMMY : No one ever falls in love with you?
NATASHA : In love? What's that?

LEMMY *grabs* NATASHA *and pushes her against a wall.*

LEMMY : There's something I'd like to get straight, Mlle von Braun!
NATASHA : Yes, Mr Johnson?
LEMMY : Have you quite finished making a fool out of me, or are you just starting?
NATASHA : Let me go!
LEMMY : Not before you answer my questions.

NATASHA: But I don't understand what you are saying.
LEMMY: Nor me, princess. I've no idea what the hell you're talking about either.

NATASHA *breaks free, unable to understand the reasons for* LEMMY'S *aggression towards her. They walk along in silence, through the corridor and to the lift.*

LEMMY *off*: It's always like that. One never understands anything . . . then suddenly, one evening . . . you end up dying of it.

They go down the lift together in silence. In the foyer they talk, arrange where to meet, and NATASHA *collects the keys of her car from Reception.*

NATASHA: Which direction are you going?
LEMMY: To 12 rue Enrico Fermi.
NATASHA: Oh, that's . . . just after Heisenberg Boulevard, on the corner of Mathematics Park. I have a car with me, so I can take you if you like. I'll get the keys.
RECEPTIONIST: I'm very well, thank you, not at all.

As they are leaving the building the camera tracks at their side. At the door he stops her . . . and asks a question, to which she answers by nodding her head up and down — which in Alphaville, however, means No!

LEMMY: You really don't want me to make love to you?
NATASHA: What do you mean?
LEMMY: You really don't know what it means?

LEMMY *takes a photograph of* NATASHA, *who smiles at him. They leave the building and drive into the busy Boulevard.*

LEMMY *off*: Her smile and her small pointed teeth reminded me of one of those old vampire films they used to show in the cinerama museums.

Inside the car, against the flashing, moving lights of the City, they talk quietly, almost unemotionally. The images are inter-cut with the illuminated numerical traffic signs and logical indicators.

NATASHA : I'm a Programmer, Second Class.

LEMMY : Natasha is a name from the past.

NATASHA : Yes, but you can only know what exists in the present. No one has lived in the past, and no one can live in the future.

LEMMY : Thanks for the lift, anyway!

NATASHA : I'm happy with my work, Mr Johnson.

LEMMY : Is it much farther to go?

NATASHA : *Karl?*

KARL : We must cross the North Zone, Mlle, you know very well.

LEMMY : How many people live in Alphaville?

NATASHA : Which reminds me; you must remember to go to Residents Control. . . . But tell me, what do you do in your life?

LEMMY : I work . . . *after a long pause* . . . for a newspaper. This Professor von Braun. Is he your father?

NATASHA : Yes.

LEMMY : It's absolutely necessary that I do an article on him. Do you think you could organise it?

NATASHA : I don't know. I've never seen him. But I'll try.

LEMMY : I've decided to get out.

NATASHA : Here?

LEMMY : Yes, I've changed my mind.

NATASHA : All right. You have the address where we'll meet?

LEMMY : Yes. . . . Tell him to stop. I've got to make a telecommunication.

> LEMMY *leaves the car and enters an ultra-modern building. He follows the neon arrows, and the camera tracks behind him to the desk, where he asks about his telecommunication. The* CLERK *nonchalantly waves him up the stairs, without a word/*
>
> ALPHA 60, *with morse-like bleeps on the sound track/*
>
> LEMMY *climbs up the circular staircase to the room which*

contains the telecommunication booths. He speaks to the CLERK.

LEMMY : I'd like to telecommunicate.

CLERK : Galaxy call or a local call?

LEMMY : Local call.

CLERK : Booth two.

LEMMY *enters the booth and examines the complex coding indicator. As he does so, a man stands up in the next booth, obviously having hidden there as* LEMMY *crossed the room.* LEMMY *senses the danger and listens intensely. The man slips out towards* LEMMY'S *booth with a knife in his hand. But just as he's about to open* LEMMY'S *door,* LEMMY *flings it open and grabs him, dragging him inside. A quick hustle and the man falls dead, stabbed with his own knife.* LEMMY *carefully closes the door, leaving the body inside the booth. As he is crossing the office, he notices a photograph on the wall. He takes out the photograph from his notebook, compares the two and turns to the* CLERK.

LEMMY : Miss, do you know that man?

CLERK : Of course I do — do you think I'm stupid?

The camera pans over to the photograph of VON BRAUN *on the wall, and then pans back to* LEMMY. *He walks down the stairs again, stopping and asking a man the same question, to which he seems to get the same reply.* LEMMY *leaves the building, to morse pips and sinister music.*

A high shot shows LEMMY *down in the street, stopping a number of passers-by and showing them the photographs from his notebook, each time receiving the same response. Eventually he is shown where to go to reach the shabby hotel that stands at 12 rue Enrico Fermi.* LEMMY *enters. The scene inside is dingy, dirty, and dimly lit, very much in contrast to the rest of the city. A number of miserable-looking layabouts are sitting around playing cards and reading detective novels in the poky little reception office.*

As LEMMY *enters, a detective novel is being read out aloud by one of the inmates.*

CLIENT : It's down by the end of the Galata Bridge where you find the Red Star Hotel . . . in no way can it be compared to our splendid . . . passages, all glittering . . . with luxury and light. It is merely a huge, tall, narrow labyrinth. . . .

LEMMY : Is this the Red Star Hotel?

OWNER : Yes, I'm very well, thank you, not at all.

LEMMY : Is Mr Dickson in?

SEDUCTRESS : No, he's not in at the moment.

LEMMY : O.K. I'll wait for him.

LEMMY *barges in, making it quite obvious he means it; he has decided to wait and that's that. The* SEDUCTRESS *does her best to make him interested in her, making him sit down on an old rickety chair as she massages his shoulders.*

SEDUCTRESS : You have some money, sir? . . . You can sit down here, sir, if you're tired.

CLIENT *off* : I want to see it again . . . and the tomb of the Duke of Montpensier. The statue of the prince is the work of Pradier. The prince is dressed in the uniform of . . .

DICKSON *appears at the cracked window, looking very much the worse for wear. He stares at* LEMMY *as if he recognises him . . . pauses for a second . . . and then comes towards the door of the lobby.*

ANOTHER CLIENT : There he is!

LEMMY : Henry!

Henry!

Henry, it's me!

We've gotta helluva lot to talk about. . . .

DICKSON *registers nothing on his old, battered, bearded face. He hobbles into the room like a tramp, with hardly enough energy to walk. He ignores* LEMMY *and goes for his key on the rack; but it's not there. He turns round and glares at the* HOTEL-KEEPER.

DICKSON: Where's my key?

OWNER: Where's my rent money, Mr Dickson?

DICKSON: My key!

The situation is saved by LEMMY. *He passes between the two men and hands a number of notes to* DICKSON, *having grabbed the novel from the other guy's hands to stop his droning voice.* DICKSON *hands a note to the* OWNER, *who feverishly pockets it.*

OWNER: His key!

It is rapidly brought over by the SEDUCTRESS, *who is eager to benefit from the sudden turn of events.* DICKSON *gives another note to the* OWNER *and orders a beer. The* SEDUCTRESS *makes sure she gets ordered too, and* DICKSON *gives her a pat on the bottom to guarantee the deal. But just as* DICKSON *has beckoned to* LEMMY *to follow him, the* HOTEL-OWNER *jumps in front of them both and exclaims to* DICKSON.

OWNER: And when are you going to kill yourself, Mr Dickson! Why don't you hurry up! We need your room for a cousin from the South.

LEMMY *and* DICKSON *walk slowly up the stairs.* DICKSON *can hardly walk, and seems either ill or sick or drunk or all three. He staggers against the staircase, as he mutters to* LEMMY.

DICKSON: You've come from the Outerlands — huh?

LEMMY: Why did he ask you if you'd be committing suicide soon?

DICKSON: Oh . . . there's . . . there's not . . . there's quite a few . . . who do it. . . .

He staggers and coughs and splutters. They sit on the stairs, under the solitary, bleak light-bulb hanging from the ceiling by a single, perilous thread.

DICKSON: . . . Some of them just don't manage to adapt themselves here . . . it's that . . . it's . . . the method the Chinese

POLICE

invented about thirty years ago . . . in Pekingville. They made an art of dissuasion.

Image cuts intermittently to outside, exterior night shots of vast illuminated modern city buildings.

LEMMY: But the others, those who don't manage to adapt themselves or commit suicide?

DICKSON: Them . . . they get executed . . . yeh . . . the Authorities . . . but you know . . . you just have to hide. There's not many left.

LEMMY: And Dick Tracy? He's dead? And Guy Leclair? Why did we never get news from you all, Henry?

DICKSON: Pardon me . . . *he is spluttering and clutching at his throat . . . he smiles . . . with effort* . . . these things happen, you know.

LEMMY: And Alpha 60, what is it?

DICKSON: Oh, that . . . it's a giant computer . . . like the ones we used to have, you know?

LEMMY: Nueva York . . . IBM . . . ?

DICKSON: Yup. . . . Olivetti . . . General Electric . . . Tokyrama. . . .

LEMMY: And then?

DICKSON: Well, Alpha 60 is the same, but a hundred and fifty light years stronger.

LEMMY: I get you. People have become slaves to probability.

DICKSON: Here at Alphaville their ideal is . . . a pure technocracy . . . an entirely technical society . . . like those of ants and termites!

LEMMY: I don't understand.

DICKSON: Probably there's . . . one hundred and fifty light years.

LEMMY: One hundred and fifty?

DICKSON: One hundred and fifty . . . two hundred . . . ah, there were artists in the ant society. Artists, novelists, musicians and painters . . . today there's nothing. Nothing . . . just like it is here!

Inter-cut with the images of Dickson's *pained, contorted expression as he gasps out the words, and* Lemmy's *permanently poker-hard face, as they sit down exhausted on the stairs, are images of theorems: Einstein's Relativity Theorem, etc,* $E = mc^2$ *and* $\epsilon = hf$*; images which are flashed between the images of the men's faces as they are talking.*

Lemmy : Is it Professor von Braun who organised it all?

Dickson : They just obey logical orders.

Lemmy : Then why didn't you kill him?

They enter Dickson's *tatty room.* Dickson *takes a couple of pills and a long swig of his beer.* Lemmy *grabs him by the collar, exasperated.*

Dickson : '*Why*' . . . why . . . what does that mean, now . . . 'why' . . . forgotten . . . forgotten . . . I forget.

Dickson *grabs his stomach and collapses on the bed; the camera pans round to follow* Lemmy, *who searches the cupboards as if by habit.*

Lemmy : Do you know who Natasha is, his daughter? Who is she really?

Dickson : Who?

Lemmy : It was him they sent to Los Alamos. His name wasn't that then. Look, answer me! . . . His name wasn't that then? Not in those days. . . . Listen, Henry . . . we'll both get out of here together . . . you'll be okay . . . but first . . . you . . . must . . .

A knock on the door interrupts Lemmy. Dickson *jumps up from the bed and goes to the door, opening it an inch or two. He tells whoever it is to wait a second. He comes back into the room and pushes* Lemmy *on to a chair and hides him behind the cupboard door. He goes back to the door muttering, preparing himself for his little theatre.*

Dickson *to* Lemmy *at first* : . . . It's a terrible secret but . . . *as the* Seductress *enters she is ceremoniously welcomed by* Dickson, *who waves his arms round like a courtier* . . . enter

Madame la Marquise . . . my cloak, Madame Recamier . . . *she takes off his dirty old overcoat* . . . Thank you, Madame Pompadour. . . . Ah, Madame Bovary . . . Marie Antoinette . . . Madame . . . that's love . . . l'amour . . . l'amour . . . and I know it in Russian too . . . ah . . . darling. . . .

DICKSON *gropes round the girl, circling her and fondling her hair as if she is a prize he has won at the fair. He falls on the bed and drags her down after him. As they commence their 'courtship' the camera pans to* LEMMY *sitting behind the cupboard door, listening, not too sure of what he should do, obviously not relishing his role as voyeur of a dirty seventy-year-old tramp and the blonde twenty-year-old Seductress Third Class. The camera pans to the couple on the bed.* LEMMY *peers slowly round the cupboard door, on the inside of which is pasted a photograph from a magazine of two astronauts in space. He watches* DICKSON *having his money's-worth. A second image of* LEMMY *shows him peering over the door next to the diagram of the formula, $E = mc^2$.* LEMMY *pulls himself to his full height and photographs the scene of* DICKSON'S *last conquest. Suddenly a convulsion grips the old man and he twists in agony. He pushes the girl back and* LEMMY *runs to his side. But* DICKSON'S *head falls backwards. He is dying. With his last breath he whispers to* LEMMY.

DICKSON: Lemmy . . . conscience . . . conscience . . . destroy . . . make Alpha 60 . . . destroy itself . . . tenderness . . . save those who weep. . . .

DICKSON *manages to show* LEMMY *that a book is hidden under his pillow.* LEMMY *takes it as* DICKSON *gasps his last words.* LEMMY *looks at the book. He leaves the room after taking a last photograph of the dead* HENRY DICKSON.

2

Exterior. Night. The lights of the City. Close up of LEMMY *in taxi, reading the book given him by* DICKSON *— Eluard's 'The Capital of Pain'.* LEMMY *talks to the woman taxi-driver.*

LEMMY: 14 Radiation Avenue . . . the Institute of General Semantics. You know where it is?

CHAUFFEUSE: Do you prefer to go through the Northern or Southern Sector?

LEMMY: What's the difference?

CHAUFFEUSE: In the North there's snow . . . and in the South it is sunny.

LEMMY: I'm on a JOURNEY TO THE END OF NIGHT, anyway, so what the hell's the difference.

Neon signs and images of the Boulevards are inter-cut with LEMMY'S *face. They take the South.*

LEMMY *off*: It was my first night in Alphaville, but it seemed already that centuries had passed me by there.

LEMMY *gets out of the car at the Institute of General Semantics. The* CHAUFFEUSE *opens the door for* LEMMY, *and he pays her. The camera pans, following his movements through the glass doors and over to the Reception desk, where he is told to go upstairs. He asks some students sitting around talking, who send him farther on upstairs. He asks another* CLERK.

LEMMY: I'm looking for Mlle Natasha von Braun, please.

CLERK: Which section?

LEMMY: Programming and Memory.

The CLERK *waves him on and he climbs even higher, up the open circular staircase. As he does so the hollow sinister voice of* ALPHA 60 *starts its monologue.* LEMMY *enters a room which is in darkness, but he is shown to a seat by a guide with a torch. He is taken to sit next to* NATASHA.

ALPHA 60: The Central Memory is given its name because

of the fundamental role it plays in the logical organisation of Alpha 60. But no one has lived in the past and no one will live in the future. The present is the form of all life, and there are no means by which this can be avoided. Time is a circle which is endlessly revolving. The descending arc is the past and the rising arc is the future. Everything has been said. At least as long as words don't change their meanings and meanings their words. It is quite obvious that someone who usually lives at the limit of suffering requires a different form of religion than a person who normally lives securely. Nothing existed here before us. No one. We are absolutely alone here. We are unique, dreadfully unique. The meaning of words and of expressions is no longer grasped. One isolated word or an isolated detail in a drawing can be understood. But the comprehension of the whole escapes us. Once we know the number 1, we believe we know the number 2, because 1 plus 1 makes 2. But we have forgotten that firstly we have to know the meaning of ' plus '.

Throughout the lecture given by ALPHA 60, *about itself and its methods, drawings are projected on to the screen, illustrating the concepts. These are inter-cut with close ups of* LEMMY *and* NATASHA. *At one point the lights go on and* LEMMY *turns to say something to* NATASHA. *She puts her finger to her lips, forbidding him.* ALPHA 60 *drones on. The huge mechanical mouth of the Computer is seen from time to time, with its huge revolving electronic scanning mechanism. The projected drawings make more of an ironic comment on the concepts formulated by* ALPHA 60, *and remind one of Apollinaire's ' Calligrammes '.* LEMMY *is bored.*

LEMMY : I'm off.

ALPHA 60 : It is the acts . . .

LEMMY : Look. I'm going.

ALPHA 60 : . . . of men that survive the centuries, which gradually and logically destroy them. I, Alpha 60, am simply the logical means of this destruction.

The students are leaving their class. NATASHA *comes down the circular staircase, at the bottom of which she says goodbye to a fellow student and kisses him on the cheek, quite affectionately. She sees* LEMMY *and walks over to him.*

NATASHA : I never thought I'd see you again.

LEMMY : Shall we go? *Taking a photograph of her.*

NATASHA : I have to go and fetch the keys.

RECEPTIONIST : I'm very well, thank you, not at all.

LEMMY : I left because I couldn't understand a single word it was saying.

NATASHA *stops and rests against one of the marble pillars, and seems almost amused as she explains to him.*

NATASHA : But it was all very simple. Tonight we learnt that death and life exist within the same sphere.

LEMMY : Are you afraid of death?

NATASHA : Of course not. Why?

LEMMY *has heard enough. He grabs the door and opens it for her to go through/*

The Boulevards and traffic at night/

Camera pans to traffic light that changes slowly, ponderously, glaringly/

Close up of NATASHA *in car.*

LEMMY *off* : We took the tangent to the edge of the circle of the central precincts! As the radio was issuing its traffic programme, Natasha spoke to me with her pretty sphinx voice . . .
pretty sphinx . . .
pretty sphinx . . .
pretty sphinx. . . .

NATASHA : Generally there are people there who are Foreign Ambassadors, or Delegations from the Local Authorities.

LEMMY : But why does everyone look so sad and miserable?

NATASHA : You ask too many questions, Mr Johnson. Because,

they lack electrical energy.

Their journey continues, and they cross the Northern Sector of the city. The signs flash and flash, and the voice of ALPHA 60 *continues with its monologue.*

ALPHA 60: Nor is there in the so-called Capitalist world, or Communist world, any malicious intent to suppress men through the power of ideology or materialism, but only the natural aim of all organisations to increase their rational structure.

They have left the car and are entering the building for the Gala-Reception.

NATASHA: In other words, we minimise the unknowns.

LEMMY: What you mean is, it's not Alphaville you're prattling on about . . . it's Zeroville. And what on earth are we going to see, anyway?

NATASHA: I'm not sure . . . a sort of water ballet gala, I suppose.

NATASHA *goes over to the* BARMAN *and asks.*

NATASHA: Where is everybody?

BARMAN: I think it's already started, Mlle.

NATASHA: Hurry up. We're late, it's already started.

They go to the lift and are joined by one or two more latecomers. A woman guest, wearing an elegant evening coat with a huge white fur collar, has a code number stamped across her forehead in bold black letters. LEMMY *looks at her cold, passionless face and sadly takes a photograph of it for his record. The lift reaches the floor they want (SS) and they all go together towards the terrace from which they will watch the gala.*

WOMAN GUEST: They don't electrocute them any more?

HER HUSBAND: Of course not, darling; you remember very well that the seventeenth electricity plan got into hot water!

Cuts to inside of swimming pool in which the gala is held. A soldier with a sub-machine gun shoots the man standing at the end of the diving-board, who falls into the water. The camera pans to the side of the pool, where five bikini-clad girls are standing poised, with knives in their hands. One by one they dive into the water, swim over to the man who is vainly swimming nowhere, and stab him to death in the water. The audience applauds.

LEMMY *and* NATASHA *reach the terrace, where* NATASHA *tells him to wait by the door. She goes and rather dispassionately kisses the man at the front of the group of distinguished, important-looking men who are watching the show. The man is the man on* LEMMY'S *photograph* — PROFESSOR VON BRAUN. LEMMY *rushes forward to* NATASHA, *who pushes him back against the wall.*

LEMMY: Why don't you introduce me?

NATASHA: I told you not to move! There are some very important people here tonight.

LEMMY: Can I take a photograph?

NATASHA: I'll go and ask for you . . . wait a minute.

NATASHA *asks the man standing behind the* PROFESSOR, *who turns and looks at* LEMMY. *He says something to her and she nods her head up and down.* LEMMY *moves forward and takes photographs, including a number of close ups of the* PROFESSOR, *who turns and stares coldly at him.* LEMMY *takes more pictures of the water ballet as the sub-machine guns fire and the audience applauds.*

LEMMY *goes up to two of the men and speaks to them.*

LEMMY: What have they done?

ASSISTANT ENGINEER: They have been condemned.

LEMMY: Are there only men?

ADMIRAL: Generally there's fifty men to every woman executed.

LEMMY: But what have they done?

ENGINEER: They behaved illogically.

NATASHA *comes up and stands between* LEMMY *and the guests and as innocently as a child asks* LEMMY: Is this not also a crime then in the Outerlands?

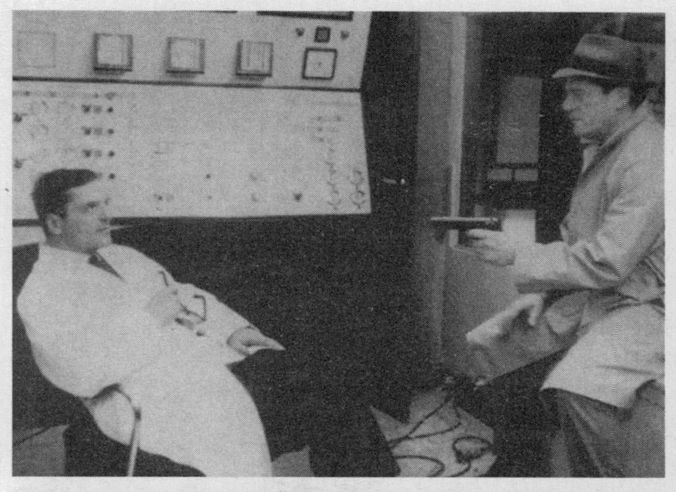

LE
GRAND
SOMMEIL

POLICE

LEMMY, *horrified, looks down upon the scene, as another man walks forward to be executed. Suddenly* NATASHA *recognises the man.*

NATASHA : Good heavens, I know that man . . . yes, I remember . . . when his wife died . . . he wept.

LEMMY : And that's why he has been condemned?

NATASHA : Of course!

The condemned man walks along the diving-board, and suddenly starts shouting.

CONDEMNED MAN : In order to create life, it is merely necessary to advance in a straight line towards all that we love.

Machine gun fire. He is shot and topples off the board into the water. The girls dive into the water and once again plunge their knives into the man's body. The audience applauds. LEMMY *takes a photograph. One of the girls is swimming back towards the end of the pool and performs a beautiful, sensual acrobatic movement in the water. The camera tracks along following her, passing behind the soldiers lining the edge of the pool with their machine guns at the ready. At the end of the tracking shot the camera pans up to the next man who has reached the end of the diving-board/*

He commences his defiant monologue/

The face of PROFESSOR VON BRAUN *surveying the scene without a trace of emotion.*

CONDEMNED MAN : Listen to me, you normals. We see the truth that you no longer see. This truth is, that there is nothing true in man except love and faith, courage and tenderness, generosity and sacrifice; everything else is but the artifice created by the progress of your own blind ignorance.

The soldiers fire their guns and he falls into the water. As the girls catch up with him, he shouts out . . . 'One day! One day!' . . . but the applause continues as he sinks to his death. LEMMY *turns rounds to see that the* PROFESSOR *and his honoured guests, together with his bodyguard, have started to leave the terrace.* NATASHA *is talking quietly to the* CHIEF ENGINEER. LEMMY *follows the men through the corridors, taking photographs of the soldiers standing guard at the entrances to the pool. Just as the group are reaching the lift and its doors open,* LEMMY *lunges forward, knocking the men to each side and pushing the* PROFESSOR *into the lift/*

Cut to inside of the lift. LEMMY *is alone with the* PROFESSOR.

LEMMY : Excuse me, Professor, but I had to have a word with you.

VON BRAUN : I never give interviews with journalists.

LEMMY : I'm not really a journalist. But can't we speak somewhere a little more secluded?

VON BRAUN : Goodbye, sir.

LEMMY : Monsieur Nosferatu!

VON BRAUN : That man no longer exists.

The lift has reached its destination and the lift doors open. VON BRAUN *steps out and* LEMMY *'challenges' him with his former name. But the* PROFESSOR'S *bodyguard has meanwhile come down in a lift opposite. They charge* LEMMY, *flinging him back into the lift, which is called by someone upstairs again and goes up.* LEMMY *is buffeted from one side to the other until, when the lift arrives at the top again, he is lying unconscious on the floor. He is dragged out and lies unceremoniously at the feet of the guests and* NATASHA. *The* ASSISTANT ENGINEER *turns to her.*

ENGINEER : You're not crying, are you?

NATASHA : No . . . because it is not allowed.

The image fades slowly on close up of NATASHA *as the tears fall slowly down her face/*

Exterior at night, the camera panning across an immense building, blazing with lights, in which ALPHA 60 *presides/*

Arrows flashing/
Interior of the corridors of the building/
LEMMY *is being pushed and dragged along one of the very long corridors that comprise the complex system of the Computer Units of* ALPHA 60. *As they march along the corridor, the mechanical voice of the Computer intones the words 'Occupied' or 'Free'. At the first 'Free' they push* LEMMY *through a door. The room is small, like a recording booth, in which a number of boom microphones and painful flashing lights accompany the Computer's voice as it interrogates* LEMMY. *An assistant, a young woman in a white coat, tells* LEMMY *to sit down. She returns to the room beyond* LEMMY'S *which can be seen through the glass window that makes up one wall of the cubicle. She manipulates the programming and teleprinting machines.*

INTERROGATOR : Sit there, and answer when you are spoken to.
LEMMY : But I haven't done anything!
INTERROGATOR : All new arrivals have to be interrogated.
ALPHA 60 : Alpha 5. . . . What is your name?
LEMMY : Ivan Johnson.
ALPHA 60 : Where were you born?
LEMMY : Nueva York.
ALPHA 60 : How old are you?
LEMMY : I don't know . . . forty-five maybe.
ALPHA 60 : What is the make of your car?
LEMMY : Ford Galaxie.
ALPHA 60 : What do you love most of all?
LEMMY : Money and women.
ALPHA 60 : What are you doing in Alphaville?
LEMMY : I'm writing a story for Figaro-Pravda.
ALPHA 60 : You seem to be afraid?
LEMMY : No, I'm not afraid . . . at least, not in the way you think. . . . Anyway, you'll never know about it.
ALPHA 60 : Rest assured that my decisions always have in

mind the ultimate good. I shall now ask you some test questions, as a security measure.
LEMMY : Go ahead.
ALPHA 60 : You have come from the Outerlands. What did you feel as you passed through Galactic Space?
LEMMY : The silence of infinite space . . . appalled me.
ALPHA 60 : What is the privilege of the dead?
LEMMY : To die no longer.
ALPHA 60 : What transforms the night into the day?
LEMMY : Poetry.
ALPHA 60 : What is your religion?
LEMMY : I believe in the immediate inspirations of my conscience.
ALPHA 60 : Is there a difference between the mystery of the laws of knowledge and those of love?
LEMMY : In my opinion, there is no mystery in love.
ALPHA 60 : You are not telling the truth.
LEMMY : I don't understand.
ALPHA 60 : You're hiding certain things . . . though I don't know yet what they are. So . . . for the time being . . . you are free. I should like you to visit the Control Centre.

LEMMY *leaves the interrogation booth. A rather scruffy little old man is waiting outside and takes him along the seemingly endless maze of corridors.*

LEMMY : Where are we going?
GUIDE : To the Chief Engineer. . . . This way. . . . Good heavens . . . the dawn is upon us.

The GUIDE *says when the fluorescent lights flicker on in a darkened corridor . . . 'Le jour se lève!'*

They reach a door and LEMMY *enters a room, in which there are two men and a girl. She is standing on the large table at which the* CHIEF ENGINEER *is sitting. It is the man whom* NATASHA *spoke to standing with* VON BRAUN *at the Gala-Reception. An* ASSISTANT ENGINEER *is sitting in a corner. The* CHIEF ENGINEER *beckons to* LEMMY *to sit down, pats the girl on the leg and tells her to go, and continues his conversation with the* ASSISTANT ENGINEER.

CHIEF ENGINEER : This is indeed a momentous occasion.

ASSISTANT ENGINEER : Yes, we have been looking for Grand Omega Minus now for three years. I'm very well, thank you, not at all. *He shakes their hands and leaves.*

CHIEF ENGINEER : Until tomorrow then. . . . And so, Mr Johnson? How do you like Alphaville?

LEMMY : Fine, if I knew exactly where I was.

The camera pans across the room to the window comprising the whole of the far wall of the room. The light is unbearably bright, so that only the outlines of buildings can be seen. LEMMY *goes to the window and takes a photograph of the city.*

CHIEF ENGINEER : You are in the centre of Alphaville, Mr Johnson . . . inside the ' nucleus ' of Alpha 60.

LEMMY : Ya don't say!

CHIEF ENGINEER : The function of Alpha 60 is the prediction of the data which Alphaville obeys.

LEMMY : Why?

LEMMY *walks round the room, ' sizing it up ', fiddling with the knobs on the three ominous-looking television sets covering one of the walls.*

CHIEF ENGINEER : No, Mr Johnson, one never says ' why ', but ' because '. In the life of all individuals, as well as in the lives of nations themselves, everything is determined by cause and effect.

LEMMY : But that is the celebrated theory of Professor Leonard Nosferatu.

CHIEF ENGINEER : Leonard Nosferatu no longer exists, Mr Johnson. You banished him from the Outerlands in 1964, and today there is only Professor von Braun.

LEMMY : Yes, now I remember. He was sent to a little town in the desert, to perfect his invention.

CHIEF ENGINEER : Banished, you mean, Mr Johnson. Today

the governments of the Outerlands wring their hands, wanting to get him back. That's why they are for ever sending their spies to us. Maybe you are another of those spies, Mr Johnson.
LEMMY: You know I'm not . . . since I'm a free man!
CHIEF ENGINEER: This reply is meaningless. We know nothing . . . we record . . . we calculate . . . and we draw conclusions. An hour ago you were interrogated by one of the fourteen billion Nerve Centres that comprise Alpha 60. Your replies were difficult to code and sometimes impossible. It was deduced that your intelligence is above average. But while in certain cases we are mortally in need of superior minds, at other times we distrust them no less mortally.
LEMMY: So! What do you propose to do with me?
CHIEF ENGINEER: For the moment we have been ordered to show you around Alpha 60.
LEMMY: Who ordered you? Professor von Braun?
CHIEF ENGINEER: Absolutely not at all. An order is a logical conclusion. One must not be afraid of logic. That's it. Period.

The CHIEF ENGINEER *swallows some tranquillisers as* LEMMY *sits at the desk listening to the logic. Suddenly two men rush in, both very young-looking, both wearing white coats, both agitated. Whenever they talk, they do so together, speaking alternate phrases of sentences, as if what they said was so well learnt beforehand, they're theoretically so much in tune with each other, that it could be as equally well said by either of them.*

FIRST ASSISTANT ENGINEER: The elements of the circuit . . .
SECOND ASSISTANT ENGINEER: . . . of 183 Grand Omega Minus are no longer functioning.
CHIEF ENGINEER: The calculating or memory units?
SECOND ASSISTANT ENGINEER: Memory units.
CHIEF ENGINEER: Mr Johnson, this is Professor Eckel and Jeckel.
FIRST ASSISTANT ENGINEER: I'm very well, thank you, not at all.

SECOND ASSISTANT ENGINEER : Me too.

Having all been introduced, the CHIEF ENGINEER *takes them along the corridors, down some stairs past a glass case in which a nude girl is standing motionless, being subjected, it would seem, to an intermittent light that flashes on and off her as they pass. Inter-cut with the images of their progress through the corridors and basements of the building are images, in close up, of small neon signs,* $E = mc^2$ *and* $\epsilon = E$*, the Relativity equations of Einstein. They talk excitedly, their conversation inter-cut with the booming voice of* ALPHA 60.

CHIEF ENGINEER : Our seventeenth Electricity Plan is inadequate. Sooner or later the Outerlands will declare war against us; therefore it has been decided that we will invade them first.

FIRST ASSISTANT ENGINEER : Directed by Professor von Braun . . .

SECOND ASSISTANT ENGINEER : . . . Grand Omega Minus will bring victory to . . .

FIRST ASSISTANT ENGINEER : . . . *Anti-matter!*

LEMMY : So that's it ! — some ideal !

CHIEF ENGINEER : We will need such men as yourself perhaps, Mr Johnson, to advise us of the weak points in the Outerlands.

ALPHA 60 : Your tendency to dwell in the past can possibly be useful to us.

BOTH ASSISTANTS : We will send men who have been brainwashed, to create havoc in the other Galaxies, causing strikes, revolutions, family intrigues, student demonstrations. That is it — that is Grand Omega Minus.

LEMMY : Where are we going now ?

CHIEF ENGINEER : Into the invisible part of Alpha 60.

ALPHA 60 : You think far too much of what has happened, instead of what is to become. . . .

LEMMY *takes a photograph as the* CHIEF ENGINEER *unlocks the door into the invisible part of* ALPHA 60.

PROFESSOR ECKEL *makes fun of* LEMMY'S *miniature camera.*

FIRST ASSISTANT ENGINEER: That's out of date, to say the least!

LEMMY: Hah! Technology — keep it!

FIRST ASSISTANT ENGINEER: Of course.

LEMMY'S *voice narrates over more images of equations, and during their arrival in the magnificent control room where he sees for the first time the major Computer Units, the programming machines, the teleprinters that record the results as they occur. He wanders round, somewhat amazed, as the* PROFESSORS *and the* CHIEF ENGINEER *fuss around the apparatus. They are obviously, despite themselves, more than a little concerned with the new turn of events provoked by the Computer's order to declare war on the Outerlands.*

LEMMY *off*: Professor Eckel asked me why I had shot the man in my hotel bathroom so impulsively, when the whole thing was merely a psycho-test. I replied: 'I'm too old to sit around discussing the weather. I shoot. It's the only weapon I have against Fate.'

LEMMY *entering the control room*: What is this?

CHIEF ENGINEER: The Central Integration Station.

FIRST ASSISTANT ENGINEER: It is here that Alpha 60 formulates problems for itself.

SECOND ASSISTANT ENGINEER: There is no one who can understand them because the methods and data used by Alpha 60 are too complex.

LEMMY: What type of problems?

FIRST ASSISTANT ENGINEER: Train and plane timetables.

SECOND ASSISTANT ENGINEER: The supply of electric power, the suppression of crime, the operations of war.

ALPHA 60: Element number seven ceases to function.

LEMMY: What's happened now?

CHIEF ENGINEER: We are at war with the Outerlands.

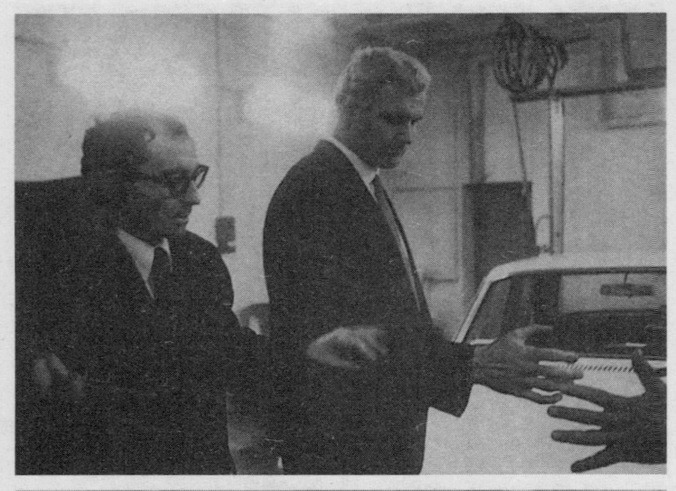

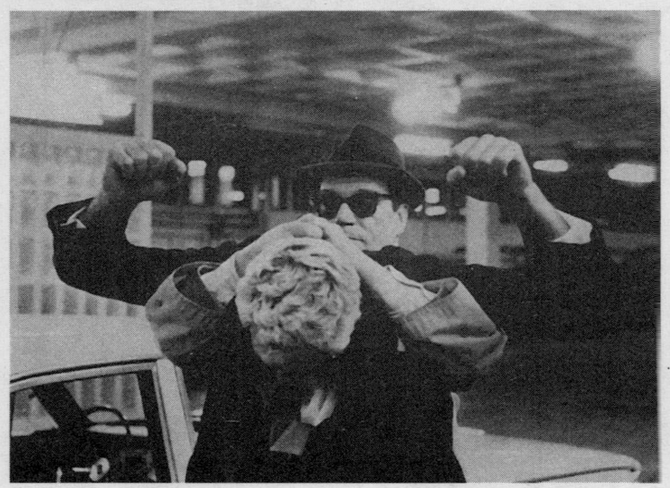

During the hustle that follows, LEMMY *manages to slip away unnoticed. He escapes from the building through the basement vaults, filled to the ceiling with electronic apparatus.*

ALPHA 60 : One single instruction is not usually enough to bring about the solution of a problem by Alpha 60. Do not believe that it is I . . . who elicits this destruction . . . nor the scientists who have accepted the plan. Ordinary men are unworthy of the position they occupy in the world. An analysis of their past draws one automatically to this conclusion. Therefore they must be destroyed, which is to say, transformed.

By this time LEMMY *has escaped from the building. His narration parallels a number of documentary images taken around the City of Alphaville/*
The huge illuminated signs/
Electrical installations through which the city is controlled/
The theatre which LEMMY *describes/*
An image of NATASHA *waiting somewhere alone close to a table lamp/*
VON BRAUN'S *photograph/*
Tall council flats when LEMMY *describes the hospitalisation centres/*
A pencil circling the word 'liquidate' on the back of VON BRAUN'S *photograph.*

LEMMY : I didn't need a blueprint of the scene to understand what was happening. In the last four years, under the direction of von Braun and his assistants, Alphaville has developed itself at lightning speed, by following the orders of its electronic brains, which at the same time have developed themselves by creating problems beyond the range of the human mind. Outsiders have been assimilated wherever possible, which was easier for the Swedes, the Germans and Americans. The others, who could not adapt, were purely and simply put to death. I visited the execution theatre where they were electrocuted in their seats while watching a show. The seats tipped up and deposited them into huge garbage cans, making way for the next to be executed. When an individual showed signs of recovery, he was sent to an 'LCC' — Long Convalescent Cure — where he was quickly restored on a diet of mechanics and propaganda. I had the impression that my life here was gradually . . . becoming . . . a shadow, a twilight memory . . . of a, doubtless, awesome destiny. . . . *Insert — liquidate.* . . . To avoid this, I had but one chance . . . escape.

ALPHA 60 : It would not be logical to prevent superior beings from attacking the other parts of the Galaxies.

3

LEMMY has arrived at his hotel and crosses the dining-room. As he is walking through a small parade full of automatic machines, he places a coin in a machine on which is written, ' Place Coin Here '. Out shoots a card on which is written, ' Thank you '. He flings it into the air, defeated by its inane logic. He reaches the lift.

LIFT BOY : Going up, sir?

LEMMY : Uhmm . . . no, thanks . . . I'm going to polish my shoes.

He climbs the stairs instead, polishing the toe-caps of his shoes on the edges of the carpeted steps. At the second floor he is met, as usual, by a SEDUCTRESS, who accompanies him along the corridors to his room.

SEDUCTRESS : This way, sir.
You're tired, sir?
You'd like to take a nap, sir?

LEMMY : Yes, to sleep . . . perchance to dream. But what, may I ask, are you?

SEDUCTRESS : I'm a Seductress, Third Class, sir.

LEMMY : Your friend — she's no longer around?

SEDUCTRESS : You mean Beatrice?

LEMMY : Maybe — the blonde with the long legs.

SEDUCTRESS : No, she's working in the Apartment Blocks. Here we are only replacements.

LEMMY : Have you ever heard about the Outerlands?

SEDUCTRESS : No, never.

They stop. LEMMY pulls aside the top of her overall. On her shoulder is stamped her code number. He seems annoyed. He pushes her aside, telling her to beat it. On second thoughts, he bends down on one knee and caresses the inside of her calf, once, aimlessly.

SEDUCTRESS : Why?

LEMMY : If anyone asks you — say you've no idea.

SEDUCTRESS : I'm very well, thank you, not at all.

Cuts to the other side of LEMMY'S *bedroom door.* NATASHA *is standing against it, in such a way that, as he enters, he doesn't see her. She is behind all the doors he passes through. He walks into his lounge and goes to the window. She comes up behind, surprising him.*

NATASHA: Mr Johnson!

LEMMY: Look who's here — the little princess.

NATASHA: They ordered me not to come here, but . . . I wanted to see you again.

LEMMY: Not me, baby! . . .

He goes as if to throw her out of the room, but at the door decides against it. He tells her to order breakfast. She is just about to do so when, as if recollecting some former self, she suddenly corrects herself, stops, and comes forward towards LEMMY, *pushing out her hand to greet him politely, formally, coldly.*

LEMMY: Since you're here, then you might as well order breakfast.

NATASHA: Yes, Mr Johnson . . . oh sorry . . . I'm very well, thank you, not at all.

LEMMY: Me too. . . . Natasha . . . bend your head forward a little. . . .

She does so. Close up: LEMMY *pushes the hair forward from her neck, revealing the number stamped on her skin in bold black numerals. He lets go of her.*

NATASHA: Why?

LEMMY: I thought so . . . oh, nothing . . . I was just thinking of something. But what about that breakfast?

NATASHA: I'd like to tele-order breakfast, please.

ALPHA 60: What is your number?

NATASHA: What is your number?

LEMMY: Don't know. They didn't give me one at Alpha 60.

NATASHA: Not your control number . . . your hotel number!

LEMMY: 344.

LEMMY *takes the book given to him by* DICKSON *and*

offers it to NATASHA *to read. At his instruction, she reads, holding the book up to her face, reading it with huge wondrous eyes, unaware of his motives until she starts to become anxious.*

LEMMY: Have you ever heard of this book?

Image in negative of the title cover of the book.

NATASHA: '*The Capital of Pain.*' No.

LEMMY: There's some words underlined in it. Read them.

NATASHA: 'We live in the void of our metamorphoses.
But that echo that runs through all the day . . .
That echo beyond time, despair and the
caress . . .
Are we close to, or far away from our conscience.'

There are words here I do not understand.

The camera tracks very slowly as she is reading, emphasising, as she reads, the gradual falling away from her logical self as LEMMY *imposes his power over her mind.*

LEMMY: What about this, then . . . 'Death in conversation' . . . and that.

NATASHA: 'Your eyes have returned from an arbitrary land . . . where no one has known the essence of a glance. . . .'

LEMMY: You've really no idea what this is?

NATASHA: I think I remember something . . . but I don't know what.

The camera pans across the pages of the book, picking out certain phrases. . . .

The nakedness of truth. 'I know it well'
Despair has no wings and nor has love
No face, do not speak
I do not see them.
I do not speak to them.
But I am as much alive as my love and my despair.

LEMMY: And this . . . 'Dying of not dying. . . .' And this. 'To be trapped by trying to trap.' This. 'Men who change.

. . .' You've never heard of a secret message either, Mlle von Braun?

NATASHA : A secret message?

LEMMY : A secret. You don't know what that is either?

NATASHA : Yes, there's a planning secret, atomic secret, secrets . . . of memory.

LEMMY : What are you looking for now? *She has crossed the room and is frantically looking for something in the cupboards and drawers.* I'm going crazy in this filthy town.

NATASHA : I'm looking for the Bible to see if it's written there.

LEMMY : What?

NATASHA : Are you an idiot or what? — the word I'm looking for, of course! Usually there's one for everybody.

She is hunting through the drawers, but can't find a Bible. LEMMY *stands with his face in his hands . . . she circles him mysteriously.*

NATASHA : I'm becoming afraid. . . . Since you arrived, I can no longer understand what is happening.

LEMMY : Me! — I'm just beginning to understand, I think.

The camera pans from side to side, following them as they move aimlessly round the room, she looking for a Bible to regain her composure, and he, baffled as ever. . . . A young man enters with the breakfast on a trolley. NATASHA *has meanwhile found the Bible near the bed.*

NATASHA : Ah! . . . here it is. *Conscience* . . . it's not in it!

The young man rushes across to NATASHA *and roughly takes the 'old' Bible from her hands, thrusting into them the new one he has brought with the breakfast. She looks into the new Bible hopefully.*

VALET : I'm very well, thank you, not at all.

NATASHA : *Conscience!* . . . Not here either!

She wanders sadly over to the window, repeating the word.

NATASHA : Conscience . . . conscience . . . so no one here knows its meaning any more . . . the word conscience. . .

But she seems to get a grip of herself, as if this is not necessarily the end of the world, and goes to LEMMY. *He has already sat down for breakfast, at the table next to a television screen.*

NATASHA: Ah well. . . . One sugar or two?

LEMMY: Two . . . *taking the Bible and looking into it* . . . but this isn't a Bible, it's a dictionary!

NATASHA: But isn't it the same in the Outerlands, Mr Johnson?

LEMMY: Tell me . . . to start with . . . what is it for?

NATASHA: Well, nearly every day there are words which disappear because they are no longer allowed. In their place, one must put new words to correspond to the new ideas. And you know . . . in the last few months . . . some words have disappeared that I liked very much.

LEMMY: Which words? . . . I'm interested.

The camera tracks close up to LEMMY *who, as* NATASHA *has been talking, is looking into his notebook and writing in it. Cuts to close up of the words* LEMMY *has already written . . . and images of the words are edited to* NATASHA'S *voice.*

INSERT: *Let Alpha 60 destroy itself*

NATASHA: Robin redbreast . . . to weep . . .

INSERT: *Save all those able to cry*

NATASHA: Autumn light . . .

INSERT: *Tenderness*

NATASHA: Tenderness, also. . . . As soon as I'm with you, I get frightened. They ordered me not to see you again.

LEMMY: Who? The Alpha 60 engineers?

NATASHA: Yes.

LEMMY: What makes you afraid?

NATASHA: I'm afraid because I know a word . . . without having seen it or read it.

LEMMY: Which word?

NATASHA: 'Le' CONSCIENCE.

LEMMY : ' La ' CONSCIENCE.
NATASHA : ' La ' . . . CONSCIENCE.
LEMMY *pouring whisky into his coffee from his hip-flask*: You've never been to the Outerlands?
NATASHA : No.
LEMMY : You're sure?
NATASHA : Yes.
LEMMY : You're lying.
NATASHA : Why are you angry with me?
LEMMY : I thought you weren't supposed to say ' why ', only ' because '.
NATASHA : I . . . I said ' why '?
LEMMY : Yes . . . and if the enemies are listening to us, they heard it too.
NATASHA : So . . . I wasn't paying attention. Because it's not allowed. Perhaps not for you, though, who has come from the Outerlands. At what precise moment did I say ' why '?
LEMMY : Another question first: where were you born?
NATASHA : Here, in Alphaville.
LEMMY : Again you're lying. Perhaps you're not aware of it . . . but you're lying. I *have* to know the truth. Where were you born?
NATASHA : Here, in *Alphaville*.
LEMMY : No, you were born in Tokyrama, the Land of the Rising Sun. Go on . . . say it after me.
NATASHA : At Tokyrama, the Land of the Rising Sun.
LEMMY : Or perhaps in Florence . . . or . . . or . . . try and discover it for yourself, Natasha. . . . *Where*?
NATASHA : Where? . . . I don't know!
LEMMY : Where the sky is the blue of Southern Seas. . . .
NATASHA : Florence . . . where the sky . . . seas. . . .
LEMMY : Or else in Nueva York!
NATASHA : Nueva York! . . . Where the winter . . . Broadway . . . sparkles under the snow, as soft and gentle as mink. . . .

LEMMY : You see ! You know the Outerlands extremely well ! Your father was banished from Nueva York in 1964 . . . he brought you here . . . which means you don't belong here.
NATASHA : This book — I know what it is. . . . When we arrived from Nueva York . . . there was a man with us. He wrote things like this. I don't know what happened to him. Here, he would have to live in one of the banned areas, where they end up killing themselves . . . though sometimes, I know, Alpha 60 manages to find a way of using them.
LEMMY : Residents Control . . . in what way ?
NATASHA : Because they are the people who write incomprehensible things. Now I understand . . . they used to call it poetry ! One believes in it as if it were a secret, but afterwards . . . nothing remains. So, when Control has an hour or so free, it records things like that, classifies them and encodes them. . . . Like everything else, one never knows !
LEMMY : Quite ! They might always come in useful !
NATASHA : Exactly . . . we're very organised.

She has been standing away from LEMMY *as she was speaking . . . almost as if to herself . . . but moves closer to* LEMMY *to tell him.*

NATASHA : I want to go away to the Outerlands with you . . . but I'm afraid. Since I met you . . . I'm no longer a normal person. . . . Tell me, at what moment did I say ' why ' to you ?
LEMMY : Why ?
NATASHA : Because . . . you know very well, Mr Johnson.
LEMMY : No I don't.
NATASHA : At which moment . . . tell me ?
LEMMY : Very often, as it happens. Last night, for example, in the corridor.
NATASHA : This time it is you who is telling lies.
LEMMY : When I said that I was in love with you. . . .
NATASHA : Love . . . love . . . what is that ?
LEMMY : This.

LEMMY *caresses her.*

NATASHA: No . . . that's something I know all about . . . that's sensuality.

LEMMY: No, sensuality is the result . . . it cannot exist without love.

NATASHA: So what is love, then?

Montage of close ups of LEMMY *and* NATASHA *embracing, perhaps dancing, against the light and alternately illuminated by it,* LEMMY *gently kissing her, a front medium shot of* NATASHA *against a white wall (as in a prison photograph) in which the light intensifies until it is painful, and then fades away again; both of them against the juke-box, he kisses her hand, she puts her hand to his cheek, she passes her fingers through his hair, and they dance ritualistically as the light flashes off and on. . . . Inter-cut are images of the police in their car, coming to the hotel, as the morse-like bleeps direct them.*

NATASHA *off*: Your voice . . . your eyes . . . our silences, our words. . . . Light that goes . . . light that returns . . . one single smile between us both. . . . From needing to know, I watched the night create the day . . . without change to our appearances. . . .

O, Beloved of all and beloved of one alone . . .
In silence your mouth promised to be happy . . .
Further and further, hate says . . . nearer and nearer, love says. . . .
Through a single caress we leave our childhood. . . .
More and more I see the human predicament as a dialogue between lovers.
The heart has but a single mouth.
Everything by chance.
Everything said without thinking.
Sentiments drift away.
Men roam the city.
A glance, a word.
And because I love you everything moves. . . .

One need only advance to live, to go
Straightforward towards all that you love
I was going towards you
I was perpetually moving towards the light
If you smile, it is so that you can trespass within me
The aurora of your arms are pearls piercing the mists. . . .

NATASHA *is seen from outside the window, holding the book against her face, 'THE CAPITAL OF PAIN'.*

4

LEMMY *in the bathroom washing his face. The camera pans from the mirror to* NATASHA.

LEMMY : I wonder how the Chief Engineer intends to use me

NATASHA : As an inter-Galaxy double agent, I suppose.

LEMMY : So it's true what Professor Eckel said, then.

NATASHA : What?

LEMMY : You'll send spies to sabotage and destroy the rest of the world.

NATASHA : Of course. We learn that at school.

LEMMY *going up to her and gripping her throat menacingly* : Are you going to betray me, then? . . . You can't talk . . . or you don't want to. *She nods her head.* Can one telecommunicate with the Outerlands from this hotel?

NATASHA : Oh yes, you just ask for the Galaxy Network. Shall I get it for you?

ALPHA 60 : With the Outerlands . . .

NATASHA : I'd like to telecommunicate.

ALPHA 60 : . . . all telecommunications have been suspended . . .

LEMMY : Ah . . . shit!

ALPHA 60 : . . . until further notice.

NATASHA : What did you want to say?

LEMMY : Just to call for an immediate bombing action against Alphaville. I'll explain later, Princess — but just now, we've got to beat the hell outa here.

LEMMY *grabs* NATASHA *and drags her with him into the bathroom . . . but a second later he backs out, his revolver at the ready. . . . They back into the room followed by the four cops who were seen in the earlier shots coming towards the hotel/*

Image of VON BRAUN/

NATASHA *leaves* LEMMY'S *side and goes automatically to stand between the policemen, all staring at* LEMMY *up against the wall.*

A POLICEMAN: Come with us.
LEMMY: Where to?
A POLICEMAN: Residents Control. . . . Get him, when he doubles up.
SECOND POLICEMAN: Mademoiselle, Story number 842.

NATASHA *tells the story — another formula — and the camera pans, close up, from the face of* NATASHA *to the hard, immobile, passionless faces of the cops, and to* LEMMY, *who is listening to* NATASHA'S *story with a naïve interest and enjoyment.*

NATASHA: One day, a little man went into a café in the Northern Zone and said, 'I'd like a nice cup of hot sweet coffee,' adding: 'But I'm not going to pay because I'm not afraid of anyone.' He drinks the coffee and goes. He drinks his coffee and leaves without paying. The owner said nothing, as he didn't want to encourage trouble. But when the little fellow came time and time again, the owner declared: 'I'm fed up! I'll get a thug to mess him up a bit . . . if he does it again.' And in fact, when for the fourth day he came in and said, 'I'd like a nice cup of hot, sweet coffee' the tough-guy sidled up to him and said, 'So . . . you ain't afraid of no one, huh!' 'That's right,' the little chap said. 'Me neither!' the tough replied. 'Well, in that case,' said the little chap, 'that'll be two nice hot cups of coffee . . . with sugar.'

LEMMY *doubles up laughing, and as he does so, one of the cops slugs him.*

NATASHA: I'll meet you outside the Residents Control.

She is speaking to LEMMY, *but the cop thinks otherwise.*

POLICEMAN: You'll stay right there, Mlle von Braun.

Camera pans across the building and down to the police car arriving with LEMMY/
He is man-handled along the corridor and flung into an identical room as before, for interrogation.

ALPHA 60: Last night you lied.
LEMMY: It was you who organised Dickson's death. Why?

ALPHA 60 : Your name might be written Ivan Johnson, but it is pronounced Lemmy Caution . . . Secret Agent . . . Number 003 of the Outerlands. You are a security threat to Alphaville.
LEMMY : Well, I do refuse to become what you call normal if that's what you mean.
ALPHA 60 : Those which you call mutants . . . form a superior race . . . to normal men . . . who have nearly all been eliminated by ourselves.
LEMMY : That's unthinkable ! . . . You can't just destroy an entire race !
ALPHA 60 : I will calculate . . . so that failure . . . is impossible.
LEMMY : I'll fight until failure *does* become possible.
ALPHA 60 : Everything I plan will be accomplished.
LEMMY : That's not certain. I too have a secret.
ALPHA 60 : What is your secret? . . . Tell me . . . Mr Caution.
LEMMY : Something that never changes with the night or the day, as long as the past represents the future, towards which it will advance in a straight line, but which, at the end, has closed in on itself into a circle.
ALPHA 60 : I do not know what it is.
LEMMY : And I'm not going to tell you, either.
ALPHA 60 : Several of my circuits are looking for the solution to your puzzle. I will find it.
LEMMY : If you find it . . . you will destroy yourself in the process . . . because you will have become my equal, my brother.
ALPHA 60 : Those who are not born . . . do not weep . . . and do not regret. . . . Thus it is logical to condemn you to death.
LEMMY : And you can go and stuff yourself with your bloody Logic !
ALPHA 60 : My judgement is just. I am working for the Universal Good.
LEMMY : If you plan to drive us from the other Galaxies, you won't succeed.
ALPHA 60 : You will not leave; the door is locked.

LEMMY: We'll see about that!

Outside in the corridor the cops are lounging nonchalantly around, waiting for LEMMY. *Suddenly the door is shattered into a thousand pieces as* LEMMY *hurtles through it. He turns on the cops and shoots them dead. He escapes down the corridor. He reaches the lobby and hides behind a screen, watching* NATASHA *being dragged into the building by a couple more cops. She is struggling frantically but can't escape. He waits until they've passed and he leaves the building/*

Cuts to negative image outside, as he leaves the building and approaches a car. He speaks to the driver and ALPHA 60 *replies. He pulls out his gun and orders the driver to take him.*

LEMMY: Professor von Braun — do you know where he lives?

ALPHA 60: At the Central Palace, to the South, behind the Raw Materials Station.

LEMMY: Let's get moving!

They drive through the Southern Zone of the city and arrive at the Central Palace.

LEMMY: You stay here — and don't move!

LEMMY *gets out of the car, and on second thoughts stops and shoots the driver dead in his car.*

LEMMY: Like that, I can be sure you'll stick to your promise, pal.

LEMMY *enters the building/*

$E = mc^2$/

And in the basement meets up with VON BRAUN *and a number of his assistants, who are hurrying somewhere . . . he tags on the end of the group and takes a few photographs. One of the assistants sees* LEMMY *and tries to stop him.*

ASSISTANT: Get out! Get out! No journalists allowed!

LEMMY: Haven't you noticed that Reporter and Revenger start with the same letter! Go and tell that to your boss!

The assistant rushes up to VON BRAUN *at the front of the group.* VON BRAUN *dismisses the group and beckons to* LEMMY *to follow him to his office. The* PROFESSOR *sits in front of the main control panel of his Organisation and talks patronisingly to* LEMMY.

VON BRAUN: So, Mr Caution, what can I do for you?

LEMMY: News travels fast here.

VON BRAUN: Of course! We are entering the Civilisation of Light . . . at about 180,000 miles per second.

LEMMY: I'm returning to the Outerlands — come back with me.

VON BRAUN: *You* stay with *us*, Mr Caution. In two or three days when the war is over I will put you in charge of another Galaxy. You'll have all the money and women you want. Look, Mr Caution . . . we are in the process of making ourselves masters of a technology so fantastic that, in comparison, the control of nuclear energy by the Americans and Russians about thirty years ago will seem ridiculous.

LEMMY: I see. You are opposing my moral and even supernatural sense of vocation, with nothing more than a physical and mental existence created and dictated by technocracy.

VON BRAUN: Your ideas are strange, Mr Caution. Several years ago, in the Age of Ideas, without a doubt they would have been termed . . . sublime. But look at yourself — men of your kind will soon no longer exist. You'll become something worse than death; you'll become a legend, Mr Lemmy Caution.

LEMMY: Yes, I'm afraid of death . . . but for a humble secret agent, fear of death is a cliché . . . like drinking whisky, and I've been drinking it all my life. So . . . you don't want to see the Outerlands ever again, Professor.

VON BRAUN: Au revoir, Mr Caution.

LEMMY *shoots him dead, fires a shot or two into the machine, which starts to behave erratically, indicating alarm.* LEMMY *slowly and calmly lights his cigarette, and as he leaves the building, he preaches.*

LEMMY *off*: Such people will serve as terrible examples to all those who use the world as their theatre, where technical power and its religion become the Rules of the Game. I was running along a straight line, which reminded me of the Greek labyrinth that Dickson told me about, in which so many philosophers lost their way, where even a secret agent could stray from his course.

LEMMY *tries to leave the building at the back, but a policeman has just discovered the dead chauffeur, sees* LEMMY, *and fires at him.* LEMMY *walks back through the building, along the corridors, through which already the inhabitants of Alphaville are groping/*

Neon sign SUD/

And LEMMY *leaves the building into the underground garage.*

ALPHA 60: In many respects . . . your reactions . . . and your ways of thinking . . . are different . . . from what is now accepted as normal.

LEMMY *off*: The inhabitants of Alphaville are not normal. They are the end-products of a series of mutations.

ALPHA 60: Do you accept our proposal? Answer silently . . . with yes or no.

LEMMY: I'll never betray the Outerlands.

During this conversation, part of the Computer's interrogation, LEMMY *is seen inside the garage. Next to* LEMMY'S *car is a guard who tries to object, but* LEMMY *grabs him by the throat/*

Beats him up montage/

And drives the car from the garage, over his head.

He travels through the snow-covered streets of the South, chased by a couple of police cars . . . a chase in which the image changes to negative/

Three cars do a multiple skid/

LEMMY *drives his car down a flight of stone steps. He*

escapes his pursuers and arrives at the ALPHA 60 *building. As he enters and goes looking for* NATASHA *in one of the interrogation rooms, the voice of* ALPHA 60 *goes on.*

ALPHA 60: The present is terrifying because it is irreversible . . . because it is shackled, fixed like steel. . . . Time is the material of which I am made. . . . Time is a stream which carries me along . . . but I am Time . . . it is a tiger which tears me apart . . . yet I, too, am the tiger.

LEMMY *finds* NATASHA *in the interrogation room, helpless and suffering, as if she is drawn towards the huge metallic mouth of the Computer by an invisible force, like magnetism.* LEMMY *drags her from the room and along the corridor . . . she is drawn helplessly towards the wall, as if only a material object can support her, as energy drains from her body.* LEMMY *has to force her . . . finally he lifts her up and carries her from the building, having addressed* ALPHA 60.

LEMMY: Take a look at her and me! There's your reply. We are happiness . . . and we are making our way towards it.

ALPHA 60: For our misfortune, the world is a reality . . . and I . . . for my misfortune . . . I am myself — Alpha 60.

LEMMY: Natasha . . . hurry . . . hurry! . . . Natasha . . . think of the word love. . . .

NATASHA, *helpless in* LEMMY'S *arms, seems incapable of realising where she is or what she is doing.* LEMMY *is trying hard to make her respond to his presence. . . . At the word 'love',* NATASHA *seems to 'find herself' again, and suddenly points to a door through which they escape. The lights of Alphaville are flashing ominously. . . . As they pass along the corridors, the lights are flickering, showing that the central organisation is destroying itself effectively. They reach the underground garage again and* LEMMY *props* NATASHA *against his car. He opens the door and she flops inside. The car drives out into the night, along the boulevards towards freedom.*

LEMMY *off*: Not all the inhabitants of Alphaville died . . . but all of them were affected. Those who weren't killed by asphyxiation or the absence of light energy flew around the place at a lunatic speed, like ants. . . . It was 23 hours 15 minutes Oceanic Time . . . when Natasha and I left Alphaville, along the peripheral boulevards. By driving throughout the night, across intersidereal space, we would reach home tomorrow.

NATASHA *is leaning against his shoulder as* LEMMY *drives; the lights of the boulevards buzzing across the windscreen of the car, and over their faces, like rockets.* . . . LEMMY, *withdrawn and cold as usual, leaves* NATASHA *to fight her own battle, and drives on into the night.*

LEMMY: Don't turn around.

NATASHA: Do you think they're all dead?

LEMMY: No, not yet. It's possible they might recover . . . and Alphaville will become a happy city . . . like Florence . . . like . . . Angoulême City, like . . . Tokyrama. But don't turn round!

NATASHA: Have I slept a long time?

LEMMY: No . . . a mere fraction of time.

NATASHA: But where are we? In the Outerlands?

LEMMY: No, not yet.

NATASHA: You're looking at me in a very strange way! I've the feeling that you expect me to say something to you?

LEMMY: Yes.

NATASHA: I don't know what to say. At least I don't know the words. I was never taught them. Please help me. . . .

LEMMY: Impossible, Princess. You've got to manage by yourself, and only then will you be saved. If you can't . . . then you are as lost as the dead in Alphaville.

NATASHA: I . . .

. . . love . . .

. . . you. . . .

I love you.

UNE NOUVELLE AVENTURE DE LEMMY CAUTION

un film de Jean-Luc Godard

Treatment

A lone car, American make, is being driven along a motorway across a silent, desolate plain. At the wheel, Lemmy Caution.

We follow the car for a little while, time enough to notice Lemmy transfer a gun from the glove-box to his belt. The radio is playing and Lemmy ad-libs to the tune.

The car turns off and draws away. As night falls we see the silhouette of a large city in the distance, towards which Lemmy's car is speeding.

Night has come. Once again close-up on Lemmy, in the centre of a busy stream of traffic. Round his neck he is wearing a tie-microphone and on his wrist a watch. Its dial is marked in wavebands like a radio and its winder emits signals. Lemmy uses it as a transmitter, and as he enters the suburbs of Alphaville he sends out his first report. He describes a few things here and there, although none of them seem especially unusual to him — the sadness and tension in the people's faces — they would seem to be living in an underground city, reached by way of ornate entrances (Métro) — and it seemed as if many such entrances were in the process of just caving in. Lemmy finishes his report with a promise to transmit every 7,200 seconds.

In this way each of Lemmy's reports can be used to compile a documentary on the town and its inhabitants. These images will be true documentary images of present-day life. But our story will sometimes deviate from their *sens primitifs* to give it a novel, rather strange, mysterious quality.

Lemmy takes advantage of the red light at a traffic crossing to ask the address of the Grand Hotel from a sort of workman wearing a cap.

He is told to take a certain avenue, Road 24, then another, and afterwards, it's straight ahead.

The worker ends with a strange type of greeting, as Lemmy understands it, without attaching too much importance to it. Lemmy returns to the centre of the very dense traffic. He progresses slowly. He juggles with the knobs on the radio to find another programme. He picks up the traffic signals telling the drivers which roads are quickest for certain destinations. Hearing the Grand Hotel mentioned among several other names like Central Station, Mathematics Park, Magasins Réunis, etc . . . Lemmy obeys the radio instructions.

A little later he arrives at the hotel (if possible a hotel like one at Munich, or Chicago, where the car enters directly into the building).

He asks Reception for a room. One ought to have been reserved in his name, Ivan Johnson, journalist.

The receptionist consults his register and says : ' I'm very well, thank you, not at all ' (or something like it, the same as the greeting formula the workman used shortly before).

Lemmy is told that a room has been reserved in his name (a name from the Outerlands !). ' You've come for the Festival? ' Lemmy doesn't answer yes or no.

Lemmy is asked for the number allotted to him by Residents Control and, as Lemmy doesn't understand, it is explained to him that he must present himself for interrogation there within the next twenty-four hours.

Lemmy thinks it's just a formality and pays no attention.

He takes the key of his room and goes up, accompanied by a maid.

She turns the bed-cover and smooths the sheets while

Lemmy paces the room, sounding out the walls with precision and nonchalance.

The maid points to a book on the bedside table. He asks what it is. She answers that it's the Bible, as given to all the clients of the hotel. Lemmy asks her if she believes in it. She replies of course she does, I am very well, thank you, not at all.

After Lemmy has gone to turn on the bath, he is asked by her if he intends taking a bath. He says yes.

She helps him take off his jacket and tie, which she takes into the bedroom. A somewhat surprised Lemmy lets her do so, expecting her to go. But she returns, finishes undressing and steps into the water to take a bath with him.

Lemmy wants her to get out of the water and get dressed again. A guy barges in at this point, asking if the young woman isn't to his liking. Lemmy says he would sooner have his sister! A fight ensues which ends up in the bath. The man flees.

While the girl dresses, completely unmoved by what's happened, Lemmy asks her a number of questions, as he too is drying his wet clothes. Who is she? Her name? Her exact employment in the hotel? (Perhaps her passivity or neutrality annoys Lemmy who slaps her, thinking she's drugged or something, but the blows have no effect on her indifference.) She gives her name, then her surname, then adds that she's a seductress third class. She then leaves with the same greeting formula used by the others. Lemmy gradually realises that subordinates say this formula after, and their superiors before.

After the girl has left, Lemmy returns to the room, somewhat baffled, and the telephone rings (another different type of ring, more like morse for example). He picks up the phone.

Lemmy is told by Reception that a Mademoiselle von Braun is asking to see him. . . . Lemmy tells them to wait a minute, replaces the receiver, and goes to look for a notebook in his jacket. We see him looking something up.

He takes the phone again and says he's coming down and

the girl can wait for him downstairs. They tell him that she is already on her way up. Lemmy hangs up and puts his jacket back on.

He takes his notebook out again and examines two photographs inserted between the pages; they are two amateur snapshots, one of them showing a face (*à la* Lee Marvin) and the other a distinguished old man. On the back of the first photograph, a name and a number: Henry Dickson X21. On the back of the second, only a name: Professor Leonard von Braun.

A knock on the door. Lemmy goes to open it after replacing his notebook and the photographs in his jacket, and his revolver into his belt.

A young woman enters, who has large eyes and a rather impersonal elegance. Lemmy asks her: 'Mlle von Braun?'

She replies: 'Yes, I'm very well, thank you, not at all.'

She gives the same impression as the maid, in appearance, gestures and a completely neutral manner of speech, as if worked out and learnt in advance. But she seems more alive than the other, as if there were deep within her still something of which she herself was consciously unaware.

Natasha, which is her name (a somewhat Dostoievskian name, Lemmy remarks, and she happens to remember this author of a bygone age), tells Lemmy she has been ordered by the Alphaville Authorities to be at his service (in the role of guide/interpreter as in cities of the Eastern bloc).

She reminds Lemmy that in any case he must not forget to present himself, no later than tomorrow, at the Residents Control. She also asks the purpose of his visit to Alphaville. Is it for the Festival? For no reason, Lemmy answers yes, as a photo-reporter on Figaro-Pravda.

Natasha says it's a pity he's come so late as the Festival is almost over, having lasted the whole of the 'passed' month (the people of Alphaville say the 'passed' day, the 'present' day, the 'future' day, instead of yesterday, today, tomorrow), but tonight there still remained a large Gala-Reception given by the Alphaville Authorities in honour of the various Area Delegations. If Lemmy wanted to go, she would take him after her evening class, as she was at his service and therefore ready to assist his journalism as necessary: his report, interviews, visits to places of picturesque interest.

Lemmy asks nothing better. He has in fact several articles to do, particularly about the scientific aspects and areas of the city, and is delighted to benefit from such a charming introduction by way of Natasha.

But for the moment Lemmy has an appointment with a friend and suggests to Natasha that he'll collect her at her class and afterwards they can go together to the Reception as she has proposed. (Unless Natasha already has a boy-friend to take her there, in which case Lemmy wouldn't like to intrude in the young lady's private life — not that he doesn't want to, on the contrary, she is so pretty, but Lemmy always acts the gentleman with the ladies!)

Lemmy's flirtations provoke absolutely no reaction from Natasha, which Lemmy assumes to be cunning or indifference, although Natasha really seems unable to understand this way of talking, or words of sentiment like tenderness, pleasure, love, etc. This suddenly appears a little strange to Lemmy. Natasha speaks with a certain inflexibility in her voice, like a recitation of a child. But for the moment Lemmy attaches no importance to it.

He and Natasha leave the hotel together, and she takes him in her official chauffeur-driven car and leaves him close to the address where he has his appointment. They arrange a rendezvous in an hour's time at the exit from her evening class.

Alone in the middle of the traffic under the lights of the city, Lemmy looks again in his notebook. He removes the photograph of the man with the inscription on its back; Henry Dickson, the name of a road and the number X21.

Lemmy crosses the street and enters a telegraph office. He

keeps turning round, thinking he is being followed. In the telephone booth, as he's dialling the number X21, a man slips in behind him, a knife pointing out from his raincoat.

Lemmy has sensed the danger. He succeeds in dodging, turns the knife on his aggressor, and leaves him dead in the box, without wasting any more time on the telephone call.

Just as he leaves the office, Lemmy abruptly stops. On the wall above the counters, among several others, like Officers of the Régime, is fixed a portrait of Professor von Braun. Lemmy compares it to his photograph : the same man all right — a little older maybe.

' Who is it? ' he asks the clerk, who looks at Lemmy as if he's mad and doesn't even reply.

In the street Lemmy again shows the Professor's photograph to a number of people who react as if he's crazy or an imbecile.

On the other hand, the photograph of Henry Dickson gets no more reactions than might a complete stranger's.

The passers-by whom Lemmy questions walk away with an air of suspicion, hastily muttering their greetings formula with a somewhat frightened intonation.

However, one of them manages to indicate the street where he'll find Henry Dickson.

Lemmy puts the photograph back in his pocket and walks to his rendezvous, which seems to be near where he is.

On his way, Lemmy makes contact with his base or his bosses (as at the start of the film), thanks to his tie-mike and radio watch.

(Maybe it will be good to show the people who have sent Lemmy to the city, talking amongst themselves and listening direct to their agent's reports.

In this way one gradually understands that Lemmy is already the *n*th secret agent sent to the city during the last ten years. Nothing was heard from his predecessors. Like Lemmy, they had been sent to Alphaville to retrace, and bring back,

Professor von Braun who, ten years earlier, had been entrusted with the final adjustments to Alpha 60, a type of machine one hundred thousand times more perfect but analogous in principle to the computers already in use twenty years before in 1964, in companies like IBM, General Electric, etc.

Lemmy, in his report, at the same time describes the progress of his mission and the anomalies of the city. Better to say 'the characteristics of the city', for they only seem abnormal if one sees them as such, and will merely be simple documentary images taken of our present everyday life.)

We return to Lemmy arriving at a scruffy café near a wasteland flanked by tall buildings.

He asks the barman if he knows somebody called Henry. They show him a man in a corner, resembling an ex-champion boxer, who still, however, looks sufficiently like the photograph for Lemmy to have no doubts.

Dickson is the first individual, since Lemmy arrived in the city, to speak almost normally to him, if only intermittently, because from time to time he suddenly seems to have difficulty in speaking — as though an incurable illness (similar to alcoholism elsewhere) defeats him, and he lapses into the monotonous neutral speech of the others or of Natasha.

In one of his lucid (normal) moments, Dickson beckons to Lemmy to follow him to his room where they can speak undisturbed.

They cross the wasteland. Several shapes pass them by. Dickson, with unsteady motion, stumbles from time to time, bumping into them and exchanging the polite formal greeting.

A little later they arrive outside a small suburban hotel dimly lit in contrast to the orgy of light in the city.

As he takes his key, the owner asks Mr Dickson when he'll decide to kill himself as he's promised his room to a cousin in another district.

Dickson, climbing the stairs, explains to Lemmy that quite a number of people who fail to adapt themselves to the new way of life commit suicide of their own free will without it being suggested by the Authorities, the method the Chinese had perfected thirty years before. Those others who don't commit suicide, who haven't adapted, are exterminated, sometimes secretly, sometimes publicly, provided they are caught, as they hide themselves, and anyway, there aren't very many of them left.

Lemmy and Dickson arrive at the landing. Dickson turns the key in his door. He notices it wasn't locked.

He's just turned on the light when someone leaps at him, stabs him and rushes for the window. But Lemmy catches him. A fight. Eventually the man succeeds in escaping, profiting from a moment's inattention on Lemmy's part.

Lemmy goes back to Dickson. He's dead. With the blood oozing from his mouth, he's written fragments of phrases on the bed-cover.

Lemmy reads: 'Destroy . . . Alpha 60 . . . by . . . herself . . . save . . . those who weep . . . professor . . . kill. . . .'

He carefully notes these phrases in his notebook, and leaves the hotel unnoticed.

A little later, we catch up with Lemmy in a taxi being guided by the voice of the traffic control. The taxi drops him off outside an ultra-modern building, the Institute of Apprentice Programmers.

Lemmy inquires at the desk. He has an appointment with Natasha. How can he find her, in which class? The warden asks to which programming category the young lady belongs. Lemmy remembers that Natasha told him she was Category Two. The warden shows him the way to a lecture theatre.

Lemmy enters the large modern lecture theatre where films about Alpha 60 are being projected. An attendant leads Lemmy to a row reserved for free visitors.

As soon as the projection finishes, the lights are turned on. Lemmy waves to Natasha, whom he's noticed in the front row. He listens to the end of the lecture, understanding absolutely nothing.

The class finishes; Lemmy joins Natasha. They leave, mingling with the evening students who look quite a normal crowd.

She says *au revoir* to two or three of them — only acquaintances, but they kiss like lovers. Lemmy is astonished. Natasha doesn't understand why: she just said *au revoir*. As soon as Lemmy has enrolled at the Residents Control, she'll say hello and goodbye to him in the same way.

They go together to the Gala-Reception in Natasha's official car. During the drive, Lemmy asks Natasha if she's the daughter of Professor von Braun, or if it's just a coincidence she has the same name. Natasha tells him she is the Professor's real daughter. But she speaks of her father as if being his child was a theoretical, not sentimental, relationship. She speaks continually to Lemmy in a neutral voice, a little slow, almost without timbre. Two or three times, she stops herself and gazes at Lemmy in silence. He asks her what's the matter, why she's looking at him like that.

But she nods her head and doesn't reply (people of Alphaville nod their heads up and down to say no, and from side to side to say yes).

Lemmy and Natasha arrive at the Gala-Reception, which is taking place in a sort of immense municipal building, as huge as an airport.

Natasha leads Lemmy up to the terrace, where she presents him to the Principals of the city.

(All this happens exactly as in a spy film where an American agent [or Russian] gets himself invited to a reception in an embassy [East or West], and one wonders if the young woman who accompanies him is a double agent or not.)

Lemmy, as Ivan Johnson, joins in the conversations. They tell him he's in luck. He's going to attend a public execution in

Professor von Braun's honour, whose arrival is expected any minute.

He arrives a little later. He consents to Lemmy taking photographs of him as he kisses his daughter, abstractedly, and waves to the people. The Professor then moves forward to the edge of the terrace to witness the execution taking place on the ground floor, at the end of the strongly floodlit building.

The crowd presses forward, separated from those condemned by metal barriers. The spectacle is televised (perhaps it would be better to view the spectacle in a special room of honour on a giant television screen).

We see the condemned in the dock which is formed within the barriers. Lemmy asks one of the guests why they were taken prisoner. He is told that the police arrested one of them because he had allowed himself to weep after some event or other. Lemmy's informant doesn't say weep; he says: they behaved in an illogical manner, and it is Lemmy who says the word ' weep ', but doesn't insist, seeing that he isn't being understood.

Before their execution, the condemned have the right to say a last word or two. One of them recites something which resembles old poems (Eluard). The other launches off on a lyrical discourse: ' Listen to me, you normals! We see the truth you cannot see. This truth is, there's nothing in man but love and faith, courage and goodness, generosity and sacrifice. Everything else is a barrier put up by the progress of your own blind ignorance. One day . . .'

He is executed before he can finish.

Lemmy, taking advantage of his capacity as reporter, tries to reach Professor von Braun, to whom Natasha has briefly presented him a few minutes before.

His insistence ends by drawing the attention of the Professor's entourage and bodyguard, who are discreet but still watchful.

However, the Professor has already started leaving and is

making his way, with a small group, towards the lift.

Lemmy follows them, always intending to obtain an interview. They arrive at the lift and its doors open. Lemmy abruptly pushes the Professor into it, making the lift descend before the others recover from shock.

Alone with the Professor in the descending lift, Lemmy apologises for treating him like this, but it was absolutely necessary they spoke together alone. He entreats the Professor to go where he can explain everything to him. The Professor seems to understand nothing that Lemmy tells him and vituperates against the audacity of journalists who believe that everything is permissible.

When the lift arrives, an identical scene occurs as above, but in reverse. The doors are barely open when the bodyguard rush in and submerge Lemmy, as soon as the Professor gets out. The doors close themselves again. Someone has called for the lift upstairs.

The doors open. The bodyguard pull the unconscious Lemmy out, dragging him by his feet. In frame the face of Natasha who, amongst the guests bustling forward to watch, sees Lemmy dragged across the ground.

Something unexpected crosses Natasha's face, an emotion, perhaps a tear, which she hides quickly, for it is forbidden.

Fade in on Lemmy, who is being pulled out of a car by another bodyguard (one recognises Lemmy's two assailants from the hotel and at Dickson's) outside a huge, superb building — the Residents Control.

They lead Lemmy through several long corridors. He asks where they're taking him. They tell him he has to be interrogated like all the city's inhabitants, and push him into a small room, rather like a recording booth, where they leave him alone in front of a ' Scopitone ' machine.

They close the door, on which a sign lights up and indicates : ' Occupied '. There are many similar doors in the long corridors through which individuals come and go.

The interrogation of Lemmy by the machine is similar to that of an interrogation to prove one's identity. Lemmy realises that it knows nearly all his exploits since his arrival in the city, and, comparing them to his replies, makes certain conclusions. But as Lemmy lies, more or less, the machine, thinking he replies as if he were Ivan Johnson, comes to nonsensical conclusions. It deduces that he hasn't told everything, but it lacks the data to tell him any more for the time being.

In other words, by one deduction to another, the machine, whose work consists in recording in its thousand memories the behaviour of everybody and everything, becomes aware that Ivan Johnson, who's sitting in front of it, doesn't tell the exact truth, as it already knows through one of its other circuits what *Lemmy* has been doing since he arrived in Alphaville. It establishes connections between what Ivan Johnson should normally do and what he doesn't do. Thus Ivan Johnson is either an impostor, or a person superior to the average inhabitant, and the machine as a consequence cannot give him a matriculation number like the ordinary people. Further facts produced in a few days will perhaps enable it to classify Lemmy into his logical category. It proceeds then to a new interrogation.

In a voice even more neutral and monotonous than those of the people, the machine informs Lemmy that Ivan Johnson is free for the time being, and it would like him to visit all the installation of which what he sees at the moment is only a thousandth part.

As he leaves the room, Lemmy finds a supervising orderly waiting for him, who takes him to the office of the Chief Engineer of Alpha 60, whom Lemmy recognises as one of the Principals of the city.

He explains to Lemmy how Alpha 60 works. Lemmy has only seen one part in hundreds of thousands simultaneously occupied with tasks like the departure of trains and aeroplanes,

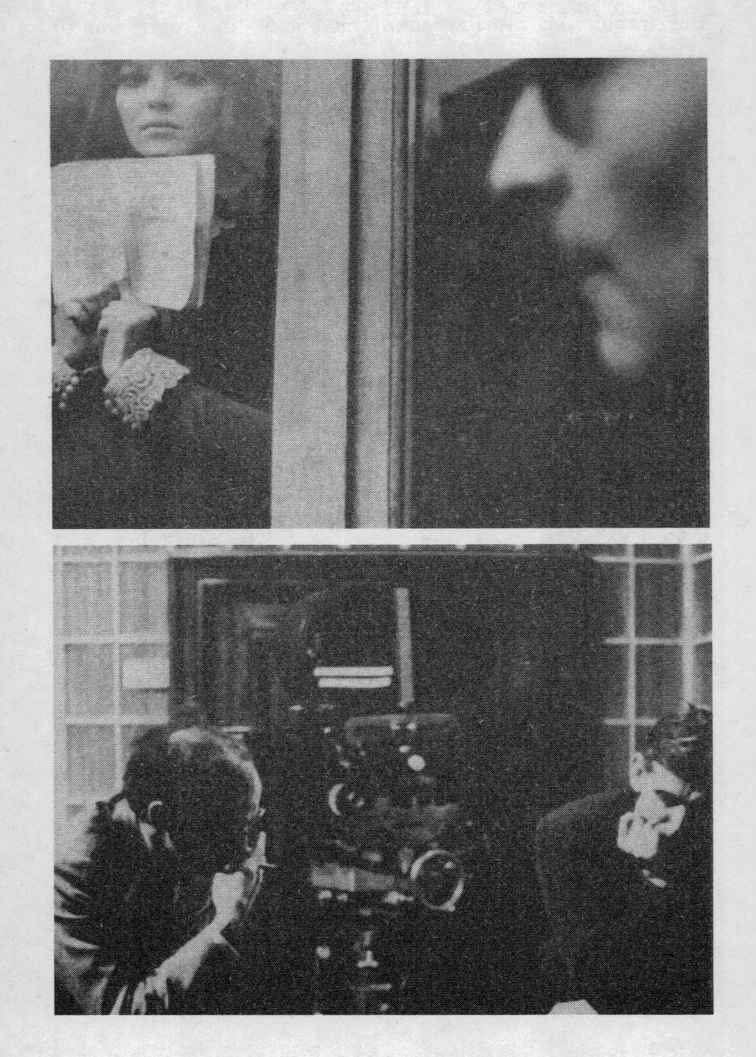

the traffic, the distribution of electricity, the repression of crime, etc.

In fact, the machine doesn't actually govern, but it amounts to the same thing, for the city obeys all its orders — that is to say, its logical conclusions.

He continues: As the machine hasn't classified Lemmy, probably because his is a superior intelligence to the rest, he can thus rise to a top post, take a place among the chosen ranks of Engineers (just like himself, Engineer Category Two, or even One). Professor von Braun himself is the only one of a superior order.

The official takes Lemmy/Ivan Johnson to another (at least visible) part of Alpha 60. He tells him how the city has developed in the last twenty years at an unheard-of rate, by following the orders of the machine. It has also developed itself at the same time by creating problems for itself when it had nothing else to do. People who came in from abroad were progressively assimilated (the Swedes, the Germans and the Americans more quickly). Those who can't be, are purely and simply executed, after a control period of examination and supervision.

This is probably what will happen to him, Lemmy thinks, if the machine declares him, like Henry Dickson, beyond codification. Meanwhile, he will be completely free since, whatever he does, every smallest event anyway will be recorded and used by the machine as so many items of data in its studies and instructions. He will be prevented from leaving Alphaville until executed or he commits suicide.

Having inspected some of the numerous rooms that comprise Alpha 60, Lemmy leaves the Chief Engineer.

He goes back to his hotel, where he finds Natasha waiting for him.

Lemmy asks her what's she doing there. She says that she has been forbidden to see Ivan Johnson again, as long as he hasn't been to the Residents Control, but she couldn't help herself.

She admits to Lemmy that she feels something very strange in him, that she can't explain to herself and doesn't sense in any of the other citizens. In short, he intrigues her.

She doesn't understand, for example, why Lemmy wanted to interview the Professor, why he'd tackled him like that, when it was simpler to get an interview by legal means.

The conversation continues, becoming very incoherent owing to the way the girl is speaking. Lemmy thinks she is either unwilling to talk or it's all a ruse. But he gradually realises it's neither.

Lemmy then discovers that certain words, especially fundamentally sentimental words, have disappeared from the young woman's mind; he asks for a handkerchief to remove the spots of blood still on his face, but she doesn't know what it is. She knows it's linen, or chiffon, but not a handkerchief. Lemmy tells her it's for wiping tears away, but she doesn't know what they or weeping are.

When the maid brings another Bible with the breakfast, Lemmy sees the pages and realises it's an ordinary dictionary. He is told there's a new version every morning with the words that have changed, and without those that have disappeared. He can't find the words weep, or tears, or tenderness, or emotion, or love.

Natasha doesn't understand the meaning of ' I love you ' when Lemmy says it to her, imagining the physical reactions between men and women of Alphaville the same as elsewhere — except deprived of feeling, and degraded, because they offer themselves in the same way to everybody.

Lemmy caresses Natasha's cheek to show her the meaning of tenderness, as he would show a child or a mental deficient, something they didn't know yet, or had forgotten.

He notices a number on the skin in the hollow of her neck. It is the control code number that all the citizens of

Alphaville wear, which the computer hasn't as yet granted to Lemmy.

Suddenly the police burst into the room and interrupt Lemmy and Natasha's conversation.

After a fight, they drag them off to the Residents Control (ordering Natasha not to move, but to wait for further instructions, when she suggests to Lemmy that she'll meet him at the exit of the Control).

Lemmy is once again dragged into the building in which Alpha 60 rules (though more brutally this time).

He is taken again into the same small room and his second interrogation commences.

This time the machine knows who Ivan Johnson really is: Lemmy Caution. Ivan Johnson had absolutely no reason to visit Henry Dickson, unless he is Lemmy Caution. From the conversation Lemmy has just had with Natasha, the machine draws its conclusions in the same way. They are that Lemmy is from now onwards a dangerous enemy of Alphaville, perhaps wanting to assassinate Professor von Braun.

Lemmy wants to escape, but the door has been automatically closed.

The police enter and guard Lemmy while the monotonous voice of the machine advises him, if he wants to escape, to become normal and be assimilated into their society.

Lemmy manages to escape the police. He dashes through the rooms and corridors, knocking down the various personnel of Alpha 60.

As he tumbles down the entrance steps of the building, he sees Natasha in the hands of the police, exactly as he had been shortly before.

He can't signal to her, as he has to hide behind a pillar to escape his pursuers.

Natasha disappears into the building, still struggling, while Lemmy escapes into the crowd.

He orders a police car to take him to the Central Palace

(everybody knows it's the home of Professor von Braun).

Lemmy forces his way into the Professor's home, where he finds him working at a blackboard in his office.

Lemmy tells him his daughter has just been arrested and insists to the Professor it is absolutely necessary to go with him and leave Alphaville. But von Braun refuses.*

Lemmy tries to convince him. But the Professor refuses to listen to a madman, and tries to contact the security forces.

Lemmy has to kill him. Previously, while talking to the Professor, a sentence had suggested to Lemmy that he might get the machine to destroy itself.

Lemmy steals the Professor's car, after killing the chauffeur, and escapes the police and cars that chase him.

He stops outside the Residents Control building, enters it through a back door, but is followed by the police, warned by the watchman.

He retraces the steps he took with the Chief Engineer up to the main room, where an operator is sitting at a switchboard, feeding into the machine the programmes brought to him by the white-coated Programmers.

As before, Lemmy bumps off the switchboard operator and dials on the switchboard the instructions for self-destruction, sabotage, fire-raising, explosives, etc.

He dashes back through the corridors, flinging open the doors of the interrogation cabins until in one of them he finds Natasha.

He drags her through the building in which the personnel of Alpha 60 have already started to panic.

After a chase through the streets of Alphaville, Lemmy and Natasha manage to escape.

The last scene in the film will be the reverse of the first.

---

* Exactly as Pontecorvo — or von Braun — would refuse to leave Moscow or Los Angeles, to return to London or Moscow.

Lemmy and Natasha are huddled next to each other in the stolen car, while in the distance is the outline of the city as it burns and explodes.

Natasha tells Lemmy that she loves him, but pronounces it as a child speaks its first words. She has been reborn, and for them both a normal human life is possible again.

★

NOTE: In the original Treatment, the Professor's name was Leonardo DAVINCI, and so Natasha's surname was also DAVINCI. Lemmy's other name was Jack Smith and not Ivan Johnson.

Godard also described his film as ' Une nouvelle aventure de Lemmy Caution ' and only later changed it to ' Une étrange aventure de Lemmy Caution '.

FILMOGRAPHY

1954 OPERATION BETON 20 mins.
Scenario; commentary : Godard.
Photography : Adrien Porchet.

1955 UNE FEMME COQUETTE. 16mm. 10 mins.
Scenario; Photography : Hans Lucas.
Cast : Maria Lysandre, Roland Tolma.

1957 TOUS LES GARCONS S'APPELLENT PATRICK
Scenario : Eric Rohmer.
Photography : Michel Latouche.
Cast : Jean-Claude Brialy, Anne Colette, Nicole Berger.

1958 CHARLOTTE ET SON JULES 20 mins.
Scenario : Godard.
Photography : Michel Latouche.
Cast : Jean-Paul Belmondo, Anne Colette, Gerard Blain.

1958 UNE HISTOIRE D'EAU 18 mins.
Scenario : F. Truffaut.
Direction : Truffaut then Godard.
Photography : Michel Latouche.
Cast : Jean-Claude Brialy, Caroline Dim.

1959 A BOUT DE SOUFFLE
Scenario : Godard from an idea by Truffaut.
Photography : Raoul Coutard.
Cast : Jean-Paul Belmondo, Jean Seberg, etc.
(Shot between 17 August and 15 September.)

1960 LE PETIT SOLDAT
Scenario : Godard.
Photography : Raoul Coutard.
Producer : Georges de Beauregard.

Cast : Michel Subor, Anna Karina, Henri-Jacques Huet, Paul Beauvais, Laszlo Szabo.
(Refused distribution by Censor until January 1963.)

1961 UNE FEMME EST UNE FEMME
Scenario : Godard.
Photography : Raoul Coutard (Eastmancolour).
Music : Michel Legrand.
Cast : Anna Karina, Jean-Paul Belmondo, Jean-Claude Brialy, Nicole Paquin, Marie Dubois.

1961 LA PARESSE (sketch from SEPT PECHES CAPITAUX)
Scenario : Godard.
Photography : Henri Decae.
Music : Michel Legrand.
Cast : Nicole Mirel, Eddie Constantine.

1961 (Prepared an adaptation of James Hadley Chase's novel EVE for Hakim brothers; failed to agree with the producers; Losey later made the film.)

1962 VIVRE SA VIE
Scenario : Godard.
Photography : Raoul Coutard.
Music : Michel Legrand.
Cast : Anna Karina, Sady Rebbot, André S. Labarthe.

1962 LE NOUVEAU MONDE (sketch in ROGOPAG).
Scenario; commentary : Godard.
Photography : Jean Rabier.
Music : Beethoven.
Cast : Alexandra Stewart, Jean-Marc Bory, Jean-André Fieschi.

1962/3 LES CARABINIERS
Scenario : After play by Benjamino Joppolo.
Adaptation : Godard, Roberto Rossellini and Jean Gruault.
Photography : Raoul Coutard.
Cast : Marino Mase, Albert Juross, Geneviève Gatéa,

Catherine Ribeiro.

1963 LE GRAND ESCROC (sketch from PLUS BELLES ESCROQUERIES DU MONDE)

Scenario : Godard.
Photography : Coutard.
Music : Legrand.
Cast : Jean Seberg, Charles Denner, Laszlo Szabo.

1963 LE MEPRIS

Scenario : After novel by Alberto Moravia.
Photography : Coutard.
Cast : Brigitte Bardot, Jack Palance, Fritz Lang, Michel Piccoli, Georgia Moll.
(Shot 28 April—7 June).

1964 BANDE A PART

Scenario : Godard from novel by D. and B. Hichens (FOOL'S GOLD).
Photography : Coutard.
Music : Michel Legrand.
Cast : Anna Karina, Sami Frey, Claude Brasseur.

1964 UNE FEMME MARIEE (ex LA FEMME MARIEE).

Scenario : Godard.
Photography : Coutard.
Music : Beethoven.
Cast : Macha Meril, Bernard Noel, Philippe Leroy.

1965 ALPHAVILLE. 21 April 1965.

1965 PARIS VU PAR. (Sketch). 13 October, 1965.

1966 PIERROT LE FOU

Scenario : Godard from novel by Lionel White.
Photography : Coutard (Eastmancolour)
Cast : Jean-Paul Belmondo, Anna Karina.